It is an honor to be able to recommend this valuable resource. As a lead pastor when we had questions or concerns, Elaine Sommerville always gave us excellent counsel and guidance. Now as a denominational executive, I am pleased to know Elaine's expert counsel will be available to churches and nonprofits throughout America.

Elaine knows how to balance the spiritual mission of the church with the fiduciary responsibilities of church leadership. As you read her book you will gain knowledge and insight that will pay dividends for your ministry. You will discover that it is more than a book to read, it is a resource you and your management team will consult often.

REV. GREGG HEADLEY
Secretary/Treasurer
North Texas District Council of the Assemblies of God

Compensation is the largest percentage of any church budget. It is also the most regulated part of a ministry's operations. Elaine has taken an in-depth topic and broken it down into detail that is understandable. This resource will help churches comply with the necessary requirements and will be a "go to" for anyone in church administration.

VONNA LAUE
CPA, Executive Vice President
Evangelical Council for Financial Accountability

D1597461

Church compensation is a complex topic, even for smaller churches. Elaine's unique gift of communicating complex concepts in simple, understandable terms and her years of working with churches make this book an important resource for the volunteer treasurer, as well financial professionals working with churches. She provides footnotes to the source authorities for professionals and practical application of key concepts in Elaine's Extras.

I highly recommend this book. It should become the standard reference for anyone who works with a church's finances.

FRANK SOMMERVILLE
J.D., CPA

Thank you, Elaine, for bringing clarity to issues that are often complicated, bringing counsel to keep ministries compliant, and doing so in a manner that is easy to understand. This book is sure to be an excellent resource for many; I wish I had it twenty years ago!

LARRY DAY
Vice President
Music Missions International

Elaine Sommerville has been a trusted source of financial counsel for my ministry and my church for more than 20 years. I look forward to having this book available to our team as an extension of that counsel.

LINDELL COOLEY
Lead Pastor
Grace Church: Nashville

CHURCH Compensation

From Strategic Plan to Compliance

Elaine L. Sommerville, CPA

Published by Christianity Today International
ChurchLawAndTax.com
ChurchLawAndTaxStore.com

Executive Editor: Jim Bolton
Editors: Matt Branaugh, Michelle Dowell
Design: Vasil Nazar
Cover photo: GettyImages.com

ISBN: 978-1-61407-920-0

Printed in the United States of America

This book is dedicated to my husband, Frank Sommerville. This book is possible because of everything he has taught me and the professional encouragement he has provided over the years. Frank, thank you for loving me and supporting me in everything I do—from family to business to ministry, you are there for me.

CONTENTS

CHAPTER-4
CLASSIFYING WORKERS
What the IRS requires for defining worker classification 45

CHAPTER-5
FLSA WORKER CLASSIFICATION
How a landmark federal law shapes the ways that ministers and employees are classified 59

CHAPTER-6
MINISTERS & THE PAYROLL PROCESS
Applying special rules consistently for qualifying ministers 69

CHAPTER-7
NUTS & BOLTS OF THE PAYROLL PROCESS
Blending regulatory and tax compliance with effective payroll systems 79

CHAPTER-8
BENEFITS – MORE THAN JUST THE PAYCHECK
Understanding fringe benefits and identifying core concepts allowing for tax advantages 99

CHAPTER-9
WORK-RELATED FRINGE BENEFITS
Structuring benefits related to the job to achieve maximum tax benefits

CHAPTER-10
LIFE-RELATED BENEFITS
Providing employees with more than cash compensation

CHAPTER-11
THE HOUSING ALLOWANCE

APPENDIX

FOREWORD

As I've directed the educational programs of The Church Network for 18 years, I've come to greatly appreciate the skills and expertise of Elaine Sommerville. So have many others in this association of church management professionals. In fact, the association has come to depend on the professional wisdom and experiences she brings to her training sessions. As the moderator for many of Elaine's presentations, I have listened as she carefully explained the principles and philosophy behind ministry compensation. She is always in demand at our national meeting.

Now, in *Church Compensation: From Strategic Plan to Compliance*, you have a resource that will help you navigate the ever-changing and unique legal and accounting standards necessary to meet HR law and accounting rules. In short, this volume will accurately direct decision makers to accomplish the critical leadership task of ministry compensation.

As Elaine gives background and reference for the reasons behind federal laws and accounting principles, you will acquire a greater comprehension of the various requirements. You will not only discover what is required but also *why* these practices are important. Following Elaine's guidance will ensure ethical and equal treatment of those who have been called to ministry.

I encourage you to respond to the resource in two ways. First, a thorough reading will help you to better understand the overall task—in all of its complexities. The Table of Content will guide you through the flow of requirements. Second, the volume will become a quick reference when questions arise, such as "Is this individual an employee or contractor?" or "Should that go on an employee's W-2 or 1099?" or "How do we handle the housing allowance and who should receive this benefit?"

Admittedly, this kind of information can be a bit dry and not the best late-night reading. Even so, you will find Elaine's presentation easy to follow, straightforward, and useful. There is now no reason to question if you got a certain detail right or debate what someone might think is the right answer based on general tax or HR law. The important answers are right here in your hands.

PHILL MARTIN
Deputy CEO
The Church Network

PREFACE

"Payroll" is a term that people often associate with paycheck processing and tax reporting. But my experiences working with churches for 30 years have revealed it is much more than that. Payroll is actually just one piece of a much larger jigsaw puzzle called "compensation."

Compensation involves every action of a church that benefits an employee. Some churches and church leaders realize this, but believe only certain aspects directly affect them. Others find themselves confused by how the pieces fit together. Still others focus on one piece, like payroll, completely unaware the bigger puzzle even exists.

One example: Ministers are eligible to receive a housing allowance. Just entering the housing allowance on a minister's paycheck may accomplish the payment part of compensation, but if the designation of it isn't completed correctly, the housing allowance loses its tax-free advantages. Another example: A church allows ministers to place their children in the church's daycare for free. But the steps necessary to provide it as a tax-free fringe benefit aren't taken, so the benefit becomes taxable.

Poor assumptions or misunderstandings can bring significant consequences. The number one reason churches write checks to the IRS is a breakdown in the compensation process, resulting in higher taxes, penalties, and professional fees to correct a broken system. Sadly, a top reason pastors end up in jail is a failure to report all their income. Pastors do get convicted of tax evasion from time to time and do end up in jail. Nothing destroys a church's ministry faster than the conviction of its pastor for tax evasion.

During my career, I have worked with many churches rectifying compensation errors. In one church, a minister regularly paid himself funds in addition to his paychecks. The minister's Form W-2 only reported his regular paychecks. A review of the church's accounts determined he was paid three times the amount reported on his Form W-2. Appropriately, the board of directors ordered the payroll be corrected before any adverse IRS action.

But Does Compliance Really Matter?

The threat of these consequences is troubling, yes. But will they really ever happen? Throughout my 30-year career, I have often heard people ask, "What are the chances the Internal Revenue Service or Department of Labor will figure out we aren't doing it right?"

In the professional world, this attitude is referred to "audit" roulette. It is a dangerous game to play. Professional standards for CPAs, enrolled agents, and attorneys prohibit professionals from providing information of "audit" risks without advising a client of the consequences of any noncompliance, error, or omission.

In response to both clients and other professionals, I often offer the following:

> *Submit yourselves for the Lord's sake to every human institution, whether to a king as the* **one in authority (and his laws)***, or to governors as sent by him for the punishment of evil-doers and the praise of those who do right. Honor all people; love the brotherhood, fear God, honor the king (1 Pet. 2:13–4, 17).*

> *Every person is to be in subjection to the governing authorities. For there is no authority except from God, and those which exist are established by God. Therefore whoever resists authority has opposed the ordinance of God. Therefore, it is necessary to be in subjection, not only because of wrath, but also for conscience sake. For because of this you also pay taxes, for rulers are servants of God (Rom. 13: 1–2 and 5–7).*

Scripturally, we are called to abide by the standards set by the government, not only to avoid consequences, but also to be of good conscience. But adverse consequences extend beyond IRS or DOL scrutiny. Operational hardships also arise. Compensation and payroll mistakes cost real time and money. These costs jeopardize a church's ability to effectively carry out its mission.

By taking time to learn the compensation puzzle, and by committing to honoring the scriptural mandates to honor God by honoring these earthly obligations, churches have an opportunity to glorify the Lord, advance their mission, and strengthen their witness without worry of government repercussions. This book is intended to help the following church leaders do just that in the following ways:

- **Helping volunteers serving on a church finance or personnel committee.** They have a responsibility for designating compensation correctly to avoid penalties to both volunteers and employees as well as responsibility to create policies and plans governing other areas of compensation.

- **Aiding pastors**, who face numerous unique rules that apply only to them and need to understand potential personal consequences when mistakes are made.

- **Equipping leaders** who oversee church **human resources**. They need information regarding various fringe benefit plans.

- **Assisting leaders** handling **payroll** because they need to follow rules for deposits, reporting, and withholding, and need to be able to recognize potential reporting errors created by others.

- **Educating professionals advising churches**, who strive to serve churches, clergy, and church employees and need comprehensive information on the tax and legal nuances for a church to avoid violating their own professional standards with inadequate and incorrect advice.

Piecing the compensation puzzle together correctly is critical to every church. It reinforces the church's mission, it ensures people are correctly paid, and every related tax requirement—for the individual, the church, or both—gets correctly handled. The activities necessary to make it happen may go on in the background of ministry, but they are still vital. Doing it well serves every church's mission because it frees ministers and staff members to focus on mission, with good conscience, to the glory of God.

CHAPTER 1

REQUIREMENTS AND RESPONSIBILITIES

The financial and regulatory requirements of managing church compensation

Many financial requirements surrounding compensation must be met on a daily, weekly, monthly, and annual basis. The compensation process requires the input, collaboration, and coordination of various people in the church. All staff and volunteers involved in the compensation process must understand the requirements that relate to their jobs. This includes those who serve on the governing bodies as well as those who are responsible for the final reporting and filing. These requirements define the responsibilities that must fit together to meet the church's responsibilities to the government and to employees. If church leaders and pastors fail to understand these responsibilities, they may cut corners, which can cause serious harm to the church, its employees, and themselves.

Government

Compensation is a highly regulated arena. The laws governing compensation are complicated, and there are many nuances and exceptions for religious organizations. Churches cannot escape regulation. Many church leaders chafe against responsibilities to the government, but Scripture tells us that we must not only acknowledge the responsibilities we must abide by our governing authorities. Here are three verses to show that.

> *Every person is to be in subjection to the governing authorities. For there is no authority except from God, and those which exist are established by God. Therefore whoever resists authority has opposed the ordinance of God. Therefore, it is necessary to be in subjection, not only because of wrath, but also for conscience sake. For because of this you also pay taxes, for rulers are servants of God (Rom. 13:1–2).*

*Submit yourselves for the Lord's sake to every human institution, whether to a king as the **one in authority (and his laws)**, or to governors as sent by him for the punishment of evildoers and the praise of those who do right. Honor all men; love the brotherhood, fear God, honor the king (1 Pet. 2:13–14, 17).*

*Remind them to be subject **to rulers, to authorities, to be obedient**, to be ready for every good deed (Titus 3:1).*

As much as church leaders may want to ignore the government, it isn't scriptural to ignore or disobey the government. When it comes to compensation, the government makes all the rules. Federal and state laws define how workers can be compensated, classified, and treated by the employer. Both the Internal Revenue Service (IRS) and the US Department of Labor (DOL) oversee and enforce laws regarding when a worker is an employee and what type of employment classification he or she receives (such as exempt versus nonexempt—see Chapters 5 and 6 for more). Employment and tax laws determine what benefits must be provided, what other benefits are available, and how all benefits are taxed. The IRS is charged with interpreting and enforcing the rules on taxation of income and benefits, including the timing and method of tax collection from the employee.

The responsibility a church bears to governmental agencies is understanding (1) what rules apply to churches and (2) the role the church plays as an employer in fulfilling the workers' responsibilities to the government.

Exemption Privileges

Setting and reporting compensation in tax-exempt organizations differs greatly from for-profit businesses. While for-profit businesses may lose a tax deduction for breaking the compensation rules, a tax-exempt organization (including churches) may lose its tax-exempt status if it fails to properly set and report its employees' compensation.

Responsibilities of a tax-exempt organization under Internal Revenue Code Section 501(c)(3) include:

- Understanding the basis for tax exemption—a church has privileges and must understand why it has the privileges;

- Understanding the ability to lose its exempt status—Congress granted the privilege and there are rules to follow or the privilege is removed; and

- Understanding the concept and responsibility of being an organization established for "public" purposes, i.e., established for the recipients of the church's operations.

Consequences

Not understanding the responsibilities of a tax-exempt organization can cause:

- Additional taxes and penalties to the church;

- Additional taxes and penalties to the employees;

- Repayment of benefits to the church by the employee;

- Loss of tax-free benefits; and

- Loss of tax-exempt status.

Chapter 2 discusses these consequences in further detail.

Employees

Because compensation law is complicated, church employees expect their employers to know and follow the rules. An employer's failure to understand the intricacies of compensation law can be costly to both the employee and the employer.

The church's responsibility to employees includes:

- Understanding the rules applicable to the church—it's a church's responsibility, not the employees', to understand all the compensation rules;

- Correctly reporting all taxable income and benefits for each employee—employees don't understand all the intricacies of the tax law and rely on employers to understand how to report compensation and fringe benefits;

- Reporting income in a manner that will minimize tax burdens to the employees—if there is a way to save an employee money, the church needs to make this determination and pursue this goal. Many times, saving an employee tax dollars results in saving a church tax dollars; and

- Serving as a third-party intermediary between the worker and the government—the church facilitates sending the employees' money for federal income taxes, state income taxes, Social Security taxes and Medicare taxes to the government on their behalf.

ELAINE'S EXTRAS

Every church has a business foundation and a spiritual foundation. Cracks in either foundation can undermine a church. Understanding compensation is important to maintaining a healthy and strong business foundation.

Often, churches are led by volunteers serving in decision-making roles (such as members of a board or of a committee). Many of these volunteers have little or no experience with compensation or with exempt organizations outside of their service to the church. Church leadership must commit to conducting a continual plan of educating volunteers and paid staff serving in these critical management and decision-making roles about the rules governing compensation in a tax-exempt setting.

CHAPTER 1 KEY POINTS:

- The compensation process entails many requirements, creating many responsibilities.

- A church has responsibilities to the government.

- A church has responsibilities to its employees.

- The compensation process requires a church to understand its responsibilities and operate in a manner that legally fulfills them.

THE CHURCH AS A 501(c)(3) ORGANIZATION

Understanding IRS guidelines for a church's exempt status

Everyone at every stage of the compensation process needs the information in this chapter! If you do not want your church or your church's executive team to inadvertently end up in an expensive mess, read this chapter and make it mandatory reading for everyone else involved in the compensation puzzle!

Basis for Exemption

Throughout my career, I have often heard church leaders erroneously say, "We're a church, not a 501(c)(3) organization." They say this because they believe a church operates in an autonomous realm of exemption not subject to any rules of government.

The truth is that a church obtains its exempt status through Internal Revenue Code (IRC) Section 501(c)(3) and must comply with all the special rules and regulations applicable to exempt organizations. When a church does not comply with the rules, it can lose its tax-exempt status. Tax-exempt status adds additional compensation issues not applicable to for-profit organizations.

Public Interest versus Private Interest

The law requires churches to operate for exempt purposes and serve a public purpose rather than a private

> **ELAINE'S EXTRA**
> Tax exemption for churches is granted through legislative grace, so despite thoughts to the contrary, churches must play within the rules of the tax-exempt game to keep their status as tax-exempt entities.

purpose. A church may have many valid exempt programs, but if it also has programs serving a private purpose or providing private benefit, then a church's exemption may be lost. If the church's assets benefit the people who run the church (or anyone associated with them or related to them) more than it benefits the general public, then the church operates for a private interest and not a public interest

Example 2-1

Pastor Charlie serves First Church. The board of directors consist of Pastor Charlie, his wife, his son, and a long-time family friend. Pastor Charlie sets his own compensation package and determines the church's budget. As a part of that budget, he has the church pay for his car, home, personal gym membership, and life insurance. The board never approves or discusses the budget. Based on these factors, First Church isn't operating according to the rules governing exempt organizations. It is operating as Pastor Charlie's private operation. Therefore, First Church serves a private purpose, and not a public purpose, so it does not qualify for tax exemption.

Private Benefit and Inurement of Benefit

To avoid operating for a private benefit, it is important that church boards and committees and pastors understand the principles behind private versus public benefit and what may happen when the principles are violated.

Private Benefit

The United States Tax Court defines private benefit as "nonincidental benefits conferred on disinterested persons that serve private interests."[1] Example 2-1 demonstrates private benefit when the church pays for Pastor Charlie's personal expenses. Any private benefit must be both qualitatively and quantitatively incidental to avoid threatening a church's tax-exempt status. Additionally, private benefit can consist of both tangible and intangible benefits or by using a church's assets. It need not only involve cash. Consider another example of private benefit.

Example 2-2

Mable Member is an active member of First Church. She is a piano teacher and uses the church's facilities to conduct her piano lessons. The church has a large selection of music, which Mable also uses to provide her students with music for their lessons. Mable has been a beloved member of the church for 20 years, so the church doesn't charge her for using its baby grand piano, the space for the lessons, and the music.

---

[1] American Campaign Academy v. Commissioner, 92 T.C. 1053 (1989).

Mable is operating her private business using the church's assets for free. There is a value to each item granted to Mable, but she isn't required to pay the value. This is private benefit.

The courts examine the benefits and the dollar value of the benefits each party receives in a transaction. If the benefits conferred on the individual or entity is significant when compared to the benefits received by the church, the transaction cannot be incidental.

In analyzing Mable's arrangement described in the Example 2-2, First Church must determine the value of the space provided, the rental value of the baby grand piano, and the value of using the church's music library. For this example, the value of the three assets is $800 per month. Since Mable is not providing any benefit to the church, then the transaction cannot be incidental.

Private benefit does not include benefits provided by a church to charitable beneficiaries of a church's programs.

Example 2-3
First Church operates a food pantry. The food pantry is open to families in the community. First Church qualifies each family as meeting the program's qualifications before providing food to the family. While the food is benefiting the families, it is not "private benefit" because the families are charitable beneficiaries of the church's program.

Example 2-4
Many of First Church's members volunteer to operate the food pantry. First Church appreciates the volunteers' time and efforts and allows them to receive food distributions from the food pantry. While some of the volunteers qualify for the food pantry program, not all of them qualify. The food distributed to volunteers not qualifying for the program is "private benefit."

Benefits provided to other persons or entities, outside of fulfilling its charitable purposes, must constitute a reasonable payment for goods or services. In the Example 2-4, the food provided to volunteers not qualifying for the food pantry assistance constitutes payment for their services. The benefits provided to workers must be reasonable for services rendered to the organization or be solely incidental to their work.

Inurement of Benefit

The Internal Revenue Code states "no part of the net earnings of which inures to the benefit of any private shareholder or individual" may occur in a 501(c)(3) organization. What does this mean? "Inures" is not a word in our everyday vocabulary. Most spell check programs don't recognize it as a word. While it is a critical concept for 501(c)(3) organizations to understand, not surprisingly, most people don't understand what Congress meant by this provision.

Inurement of benefit is an egregious form of private benefit involving persons controlling or influencing the church. Its mere existence can cause the loss of a church's tax-exempt status, and it need not be substantial or material in nature to threaten that status.

ELAINE'S EXTRA

Despite the potential for extremely negative consequences, most people, including professionals, do not understand the consequences or the costs of inurement of benefit. Without diligence, inurement can exist in any church due to weak compensation practices.

In Example 2-1, the personal benefits for Pastor Charlie not only create private benefit, but they rise to the level of inurement of benefit since Pastor Charlie is a director and senior pastor of First Church. In Example 2-2, the arrangement with Mable could be inurement of benefit if Mable were a member of the church's finance committee or board or related to any of those persons.

Originally, the law didn't provide for many ways to punish the persons participating in inurement of benefit. The law allowed for an organization to lose its tax-exempt status, but the people who caused the problem risked suffering few consequences for their behavior. However, in 1995 Congress enacted IRC Section 4958, which creates a system of sanctions for persons involved in inurement of benefit transactions in addition to the threat of revocation of tax-exempt status to the organization. These individual sanctions are discussed later in this chapter.

Not Like For-Profit Organizations

A specific area of concern for potential private benefit or inurement of benefit involves compensation arrangements.

For a taxable organization, paying unreasonable compensation or providing a taxable fringe benefit that is improperly reported may result in the loss of an income tax deduction or higher taxes, and some penalties and interest. In the for-profit world, only in extreme cases is paying unreasonable compensation life-threatening to a business.

By contrast, in a church, paying unreasonable compensation or failing to report a taxable fringe benefit properly may create a private benefit or inurement of benefit. Not only does a church risk additional taxes, interest, and penalties, but improper reporting of compensation may threaten the life of the church. It may result in the church losing its tax-exempt status and/or the assessment of sanctions against directors, committee members, pastors, and other key church employees.

Inurement, Excess Benefit Transactions, and Intermediate Sanctions

Inurement of benefit poses a serious threat to the church's tax exemption, and since no de minimis threshold exists (meaning *any* amount constituting a violation may threaten the church's tax-exempt status), Congress provided the IRS with a financial tool to punish people participating in inurement of benefit without having to punish the church. That occurred through a sanctions scheme established through IRC Section 4958.

Excess Benefit Transaction

An excess benefit transaction is any transaction involving a "disqualified person" in which the benefit provided by the church is greater than the benefit received by the church. In other words, the church gives more than it gets from a transaction. The "excess" is the amount subject to correction and sanctions.

Disqualified Person

A disqualified person is a person of influence in an organization, either currently or within the past five years. There are several categories of persons with presumed influence who are considered "disqualified":

> **ELAINE'S EXTRA**
>
> An excess benefit may occur in other areas outside of compensation. For example, transactions involving the sale or purchase of property, or the use of property owned by the church, may create an excess benefit transaction.

- Members of the governing body, including members of committees working in areas of significant influence within the church;

- Officers;

- Top management officials, such as pastoral staff (especially the senior pastor);

- Family members of the above groups, which includes spouses; brothers and sisters; spouses of brothers or sisters; parents, grandparents, or other ancestors; children; grandchildren; great-grandchildren; and spouses of children, grandchildren, and great-grandchildren; and

- Entities in which 35 percent or more is controlled by the above persons.

Other people may also be disqualified persons, even if they don't strictly fit into one of the above categories. Any person who can make significant decisions or exert significant control within the organization may be deemed a disqualified person.

Correction and Sanctions

Excess benefit transactions require resolution and have consequences.

Correction

If an excess benefit transaction occurrs, the transaction must be "corrected." Correction requires the individual to return the amount of the excess benefit transaction (the "extra") plus interest to the church. The goal is to return the church back to the place it was before the transaction occurred.

Consequences

At the point the excess benefit transaction occurred, it is subject to sanctions or taxes. Technically, a transaction cannot be undone; it may only be corrected. The individual must self-assess and pay the sanction to the IRS. Correction of the transaction does not avoid the sanctions.

The sanctions—also called penalties or excise taxes—involve the following:

- Person benefiting from the excess benefit transaction[2]:

  › 25 percent of the initial transaction; and/or

  › 200 percent of the initial transaction, if

ELAINE'S EXTRA

A good rule of thumb for determining who is a disqualified person is to determine who the movers, shakers, and decision-makers are in the church and then add in their family members and any organizations they own.

ELAINE'S EXTRA

Excess benefit transactions are not to be taken lightly within the church world. A case involving a church leader illustrates this point. In *TAM 200435020*, the head of a church was held jointly and severally liable for the sanctions assessed to other disqualified persons since he had authority over all the church's expenditures.

---

[2] IRC Section 4958(a)(1) &(b)

the transaction is not corrected by the time Form 4720 is filed reporting the excess benefit transaction or by the time the IRS issues a notice of deficiency.

- Persons agreeing to the transaction generating the excess benefit transaction[3] may also be assessed a sanction, underscoring why individuals shouldn't agree to these transactions simply out of respect for a disqualified person. The consequences are too great:

  › 10 percent of the initial transaction not to exceed $20,000.

If more than one person is liable for any sanction, then all people shall be jointly and severally liable for such tax.[4]

Excess Benefit Transactions and Compensation

An excess benefit transaction is created when a church pays a worker more than is reasonable for the services rendered, or when the church fails to report a taxable fringe benefit.

Example 2-5
Buddy is the business administrator of First Church. He also serves as the treasurer of First Church. The personnel committee agrees to pay Buddy $75,000 per year for his services to the church. Committee members think this is a fair amount and he needs this amount to cover all his annual expenses. Outside salary surveys, however, indicate the reasonable compensation for Buddy's services at comparable churches is $65,000. Unfortunately, this arrangement creates an excess benefit transaction of $10,000 without any other justification for the additional $10,000.

Consequences:

- The excess benefit of $10,000 must be repaid to the church.

- Buddy must file Form 4720 to report the excess benefit to the IRS and pay a sanction of $2,500 to the IRS (25 percent of the initial transaction).

- First Church should file Form 4720 to report the members of the personnel committee for agreeing to the excess benefit transaction and have them jointly pay a sanction of $1,000 (10 percent of the initial transaction divided among them based on their level of responsibility with the decision).

---

[3] IRC Section 4958(a)(2)
[4] IRC Section 4958(d)(1)

The Rebuttable Presumption—A Pattern for Protection

Realizing the above scenario for Buddy and others might be difficult to determine and administrate, Congress provided a rebuttable presumption[5] to assist in creating an objective measure of a transaction. Sometimes called a "safe harbor," the statute allows the church to presume a transaction is reasonable. In the realm of compensation setting, no excess benefit is created if these three factors are present:

Comparable Data

The church must base the transaction on outside comparable data. For compensation, this includes outside compensation surveys, individual compensation studies, or direct comparisons with other organizations. (Direct comparisons have limited reliability and should be cautiously utilized by churches with more than $1 million in annual revenue. This is further discussed in Chapter 3.)

Independent Decision-Makers

The transaction must be approved, in advance, by the properly authorized body and by persons who are both independent to the transaction and independent of the person involved in the transaction. A person is independent if:

- The person is not participating or benefiting from the transaction, or is not a family member of the disqualified person subject to the transaction. For instance, a pastor cannot vote on his or her own compensation, nor can any of his or her family members vote on his or her compensation;

- The person is not in an employment relationship or receiving compensation or other payments subject to the control of this disqualified person. For instance, a person under the supervision of the pastor, or whose compensation might be set by the pastor, cannot vote on the pastor's compensation; or

- The person will not have a transaction providing an economic benefit subject to the approval of this disqualified person. For instance, a CPA serving on the finance committee cannot vote on the pastor's compensation if the pastor can decide whether to use or not use the CPA for the church's accounting services.

Documentation

The church must document any approval of the transaction in writing, including all supporting information. Documentation must include:

---

[5] Treas. Reg. Section 53.4958-6

- The terms of the transaction and the date it was approved;

- The members of the authorized body present during the discussion of the transaction and those who voted on the transaction;

- A description of the comparable data and how the authorized body utilized it; and

- Disclosure of everyone who possessed a potential conflict of interest and how the authorized body addressed it.

Example 2-6

Doug Doright, a member of the personnel committee of First Church, attended the Ultimate Financial & Legal Seminar™ this year and realized there may be issues with Buddy's compensation package of $75,000. Since the $75,000 package wasn't supported by the salary survey of $65,000, he encourages the church to hire a compensation expert to provide an independent salary report for Buddy and his position. The salary report supports a salary range for Buddy's position at First Church as $70,000 to $80,000. After addressing any potential conflicts of interests and reviewing the expert' report, the personnel committee recorded its deliberation and decision to compensate Buddy $75,000 in its minutes.

> **ELAINE'S EXTRA**
>
> A transaction that creates an excess benefit transaction can result in a penalty to the people who agreed to the transaction. If a decision-maker does not agree with the compensation being approved, he must make sure his "no" vote is recorded in the written documentation.

Result:

First Church now meets the rebuttable presumption, so an excess benefit transaction is not created and it avoids all the sanctions in Example 2-5 on page 29.

Failing one or more of the three prongs of the rebuttable presumption does not automatically create an excess benefit transaction. However, it places the burden of proof on the church to prove the excess benefit transaction does not exist. The church's failure to meet the rebuttable presumption requirements may make it more difficult to prove it acted reasonably in approving the transaction.

The Automatic Excess Benefit Transaction

A church can take all the proper steps to establish a compensation package and still run afoul of the excess benefit transaction rules in other areas of compensation. Faulty documentation and failure to report other taxable fringe benefits may create an automatic excess benefit. To avoid creating an automatic excess benefit transaction, a church must indicate, through contemporaneous documentation, that it intends for the benefit to constitute compensation for performing services.[6] (See Chapter 3 for a definition of contemporaneous substantiation.)

Example 2-7

First Church properly documents Buddy's compensation package of $75,000 cash compensation with the provision of health insurance. During the year, Buddy instructs the church's bookkeeper to pay his annual life insurance premium. He tells the bookkeeper he discussed this with the chair of the personnel committee, who agrees payment of the premium seems reasonable to him. The bookkeeper pays the insurance premium, but at the end of the year she does not report it on Buddy's Form W-2 in Box 1 as part of his taxable compensation. Since First Church did not contemporaneously document approval of the life insurance premium, and since the church did not include the premium on Buddy's Form W-2, the life insurance premium is an automatic excess benefit transaction. Buddy is subject to the sanctions and corrections previously discussed in this chapter.

ELAINE'S EXTRA

Written minutes are a necessary element of strong governance practices. Churches who do not require financial-oriented committees to keep minutes are weakening the church's governance structure. In the event of an IRS examination, one of the first documents requested is the organizational minutes.

Example 2-8

It is tax time and Buddy takes all his information to his CPA to prepare his annual tax return. During their conversations, Buddy mentions the life insurance premium paid by the church. His CPA tells him that the premium is taxable and should have been reported on his Form W-2. The CPA contacts the church and assists the bookkeeper in filing a corrected Form W-2 to include the premium in Buddy's taxable income. The CPA then files Buddy's tax return using the corrected information. The contemporaneous documentation standard has now been met and the premium no longer creates an excess benefit transaction. There are no consequences to the church or to Buddy.

The possibility of automatic excess benefit transactions requires churches to understand all aspects of compensation, from the initial steps of determining compensation through the

---

[6] Treas. Reg. Section 53.4958-4(c)

final steps of reporting compensation. Since not everyone may be involved in every aspect, churches must set up policies and procedures to assist each person in communicating with the other persons involved in compensation. For example, if First Church's policies instruct the bookkeeper to be provided documentation from the personnel committee prior to paying for any benefit, or if she had been trained in identifying and reporting benefits so the benefit was reported on the Form W-2, the potential for an automatic excess benefit transaction is decreased. Maintaining a relationship with, and seeking advice from, a qualified tax professional also assists churches in avoiding automatic excess benefit transactions.

CHAPTER 2 KEY POINTS:

- Churches are 501(c)(3) organizations and must play by the rules.

- Church assets cannot be used for the personal purposes of individuals.

- People who use a church's assets inappropriately may threaten the church's tax-exempt status and be subject to cash sanctions.

- Compensation must be reasonable for the services performed for the church.

- Churches must understand the steps to create and document reasonable compensation packages.

- Churches must document all aspects of compensation.

- Excess benefit transactions may be inadvertently created by tax reporting failures.

REASONABLE COMPENSATION

Addressing the legal, social, and market dynamics affecting pay and benefits

Sometimes it seems the only unreasonable compensation in churches is unreasonably low compensation. Many churches cannot afford to pay market rates for the talent to lead and maintain their operations, and the idea that churches may set compensation too high seems like a foreign concept.

However, the American church landscape is changing. The megachurch, multisite church, and international church movements require advanced skills, and these specializations usually come at a price. Even churches not falling into one of the three movements face challenges in filling skilled positions. Small- and mid-sized congregations are more involved in technology and other operations requiring specializations. Senior pastors, regardless of church size, face decision-making and management responsibilities today that are more akin to the duties of a chief executive officer, rather than those handled by the senior pastors of yesteryear. The expectations that come with these expanded responsibilities, and the skills necessary to meet these expectations, are changing the church landscape.

Complicating matters further: Churches not only compete with each other for talent, but also increasingly compete with other nonprofit and for-profit employers to attract and retain it.

Consequently, churches increasingly feel obliged to pay more, contemplating arrangements that move pastors and staff toward the upper ends of the pay scale. However, as "reasonable compensation" now encompasses legal connotations as well as social and market connotations, it is important to remember that even churches with small or modest budgets can still violate IRS rules related to compensation. Special bonuses, tuition assistance, and other seemingly "low-cost" ways of financially blessing leaders can trigger penalties.

In short, regardless of size and setting, if leaders are not cautious with how they handle payments and transactions for pastors and staff, problems can arise.

High Stakes

Outside of market or social considerations, setting reasonable compensation for tax-compliance purposes is required for both for-profit businesses and churches alike. But a significant difference between businesses and churches is the potential tax consequences. Businesses usually can keep operating, even when they run afoul of the tax rules. Churches, however, face tax penalties and the loss of tax exemption (as discussed in Chapter 2), both of which can threaten their very existence.

Given the high stakes, the task of determining reasonable compensation in churches becomes critical. And it includes both objective and subjective analyses, shaped by individual circumstances for each church.

There are a number of tools—such as compensation comparisons from other churches—available to help church leaders set reasonable compensation packages. These tools are a crucial starting point, because once reasonable compensation for a position is determined, it becomes foundational for developing a compensation plan. This determination creates the overall cap on what may be offered to a worker. Metaphorically, this cap serves as the umbrella under which all payments and benefits must fit in order to meet IRS requirements.

ELAINE'S EXTRA

Even if performed for tax compliance reasons, determining reasonable compensation of key staff positions provides decision-makers with a realistic view of what church employees are worth for the talent and experience they bring to the table, and creates a greater appreciation for employees, no matter the final pay arrangement.

While not specifically establishing a maximum compensation amount for nonprofit organizations, Congress enacted a new excise tax on compensation packages exceeding $1 million. Nonprofit organizations are now required to pay an excise tax on remuneration paid in excess of $1 million to a covered employee.[1] A covered employee is one of the five highest-compensated employees of the organization for the current taxable year. Remuneration is compensation paid, which is subject to federal income tax withholding. While the law excludes payments for certain medical professionals, it does not provide any

---

[1] IRC Section 4960

other specific exclusions. Therefore, the new law applies to churches. However, compensation paid to a minister is not compensation subject to federal income tax withholding. Due to this special definition in the tax code, compensation paid to a minister is not subject to the new excise tax, even if it is in excess of $1 million.

Let's look at how the process should go.

Components to Build Reasonable Compensation

A church can pay any amount up to a reasonable point for any employment position. Due to potential excess benefit transactions (discussed in Chapter 2), a church must formally analyze compensation paid to certain staff members in key decision-making positions—normally the senior pastor and any other senior leadership. But as a best practice, a church really should perform this analysis on all compensated positions.

Several factors should be evaluated for this analysis.

Outside Data

Data compiled by independent sources is the most important factor. This outside data is often the best validation to justify an amount paid. The three primary sources for outside data are as follows:

- **Salary surveys.** Church compensation arrangements are not public information like they are for other nonprofits. However, there are several organizations that regularly conduct church salary surveys (including Church Law & Tax's ChurchSalary.com). The information comes from churches that have voluntarily agreed to participate in a survey and provide compensation data. The data often cover such factors as position, size of congregation, location, cash compensation, and benefits.

  There are pros and cons to salary surveys.

  The pros:

  > Established surveys are readily available;

  > The data provided is easy to understand; and

  > Government regulators like salary surveys.

  The cons:

  > The surveys available tend to represent more smaller churches than larger churches,

which limits their usefulness for larger churches;

› Higher-paying churches tend not to participate in the surveys because they do not want to stand out from those lower-paying churches;

› Surveys tend not to consider a person's unique talents and work experience; and

› Little consideration is given to the complexity of each reporting church.

A church does not need to limit its outside data to church salary surveys. There are other salary surveys for nonprofits (such as hospitals, social service organizations, and so on). These surveys have a broader pool of data and the information often is available to the public.

Consulting salary data from secular studies is also useful for positions with equivalent positions in the secular work force. For example, if a church hires a graphic designer, the best comparable data may come from secular sources, rather than the typical church salary survey.

> **ELAINE'S EXTRA**
> Participating in salary surveys is beneficial to the whole church community. Churches of all sizes need to participate to assist in creating stronger results from the surveys. Currently, small- to mid-sized organizations benefit the most from these surveys.

Even for traditional church positions, secular surveys may provide more useful data due to the complexity of the church. A senior pastor of a multi-million dollar church easily may be more appropriately compared to a secular business of a similar size and operating budget than to a typical church.

• **Independent salary consultants.** Many independent salary consultants are available to assist with compensation reports for specific positions. Salary consultants provide excellent information in determining compensation where a salary survey is inadequate.

Churches that would like to hire a salary consultant should look for one experienced in working with the church community. Qualified salary consultants perform these services on a full-time, professional basis and have specialized training and experience in human resources and compensation planning. The qualified consultant relies on, and presents at least, three to five unrelated data sources as part of his or her analysis.

When assessing the validity of the data used to determine reasonable compensation, government regulators scrutinize a salary consultant's credentials, as well as the methodology and data used by the consultant to support his or her conclusions. Courts have rejected information from consultants who used faulty or irrelevant data.[2]

Also note: Many attorneys and CPAs may work with churches, but that doesn't qualify them as a professional in compensation planning and consulting. These professionals may provide valuable assistance with a compensation-setting process, but they should not be the sole expert relied upon to determine a reasonable amount of compensation. Most CPAs and attorneys lack formal training in human resources management and setting compensation for workers.

- **Comparisons with other churches.** Churches averaging less than $1 million in annual revenue may compare data from three other similar churches or organizations, according to the IRS code.[3] Larger churches may use an actual comparison method, but there is no set number of similar organizations that must be used for the data to be relevant.

Other Important Factors

Church leaders should also consider these other key factors when they evaluate reasonable compensation:

- **Size and complexity of the church.** Churches come in different shapes and sizes and require different skills due to different levels of complexity. A church with one location is managed differently from a multi-site church. A church with extensive television or internet activities, for example, requires different talents than a church without media activities.

- **Mission of the church.** A church's activities may be focused within the local community or internationally. Mission focus may be traditional church activities or may include operating parachurch organizations, such as a crisis pregnancy center, a drug rehabilitation center, or a Bible school. The size and scope of these activities may influence responsibilities carried by pastors and staff, and thus affect what they get paid.

- **Location.** The cost of living varies widely by region and may factor into compensation decisions. Care should be taken when considering this factor, as a high cost of living does not automatically support a high compensation package. This factor should be applied after determining reasonable compensation using national compensation data.

- **Employee's qualifications.** This is always a factor in determining compensation. A less-experienced or less-qualified employee does not command the same salary as one with greater experience or better qualifications.

---

[2] Hendricks Furniture, Inc., TC Memo, 1099-133
[3] Treas. Reg. Section 53-4958-6(c)(ii)

- **Nature and scope of the employment duties.** Levels of responsibility assigned to the employee should be reviewed, including the number of work hours required, supervisory responsibility, and decision-making responsibility.

- **The prevailing economic conditions of the area.** While tightly aligned with location, the local economy may drive compensation.

- **The overall salary philosophy of the church.** Every church has a salary philosophy—it may be stated or it may exist in an underlying manner. The salary philosophy should be in a policy adopted by the church governing body. The philosophy must be applied across the board to all positions. For example, paying the senior pastor at the 80th percentile as determined by the compensation study while paying the rest of the staff at the 50th percentile will create doubt as to the reasonableness of the senior pastor's compensation.

> **ELAINE'S EXTRA**
>
> Do not base compensation on a percentage of revenues unless it is subject to a cap of predetermined reasonable compensation. Open-ended percentage compensation arrangements are considered abusive and unreasonable by the IRS.

Outside of ministerial positions, a church is subject to most federal and state nondiscrimination rules. This means some churches' salary philosophies may not be lawful. For example, a church that pays men more than women—based on a view that men are the primary breadwinners of a household—may be illegal. Or a church can have a salary philosophy that is racially discriminatory. Caution must be given to any of these underlying philosophies, taking care to ensure the church does not violate any federal or state employment laws. Other salary philosophies may center on whether the church pays market rates or below-market rates. And, any lawful salary philosophy a church maintains also must be reflected throughout all positions in the church—the church should not set compensation based on one philosophy for its pastoral staff, then use a different one for nonministerial staff, for instance.

- **The financial condition of the church.** Consider the overall financial position of the church and not just annual revenue. Some questions to consider: Is the church carrying a high amount of debt? Is it capable of meeting all its financial obligations? Does it operate comfortably within its budget?

Take all these factors into account, along with salary data, to determine the upper limit of reasonable compensation for church employees.

Reasonable Compensation—The Umbrella

I mentioned earlier the idea of reasonable compensation as an umbrella. Once the reasonable amount is determined for a position, it becomes the umbrella used to evaluate all compensation that will fall under it, including all benefits provided by the church in exchange for performing services (both cash and noncash benefits, taxable and nontaxable).[4] A church may choose not to pay the full amount it identifies, but it must not exceed this amount.

Identify the Benefits

A regular paycheck does not show the complete picture of all the benefits an employee receives. As detailed in Chapter 2, reasonable compensation does not stop at the analysis of cash. Everything benefiting the employee is key and must be reviewed. This includes all forms of salaries, fees, bonuses, deferred compensation, contributions to qualified retirement plans, medical plans, dental plans, life insurance, severance pay, disability benefits, housing allowance, other allowances, expense reimbursements (except for accountable expense reimbursement plans), automobiles, tuition, and any other benefits. Anything benefiting an employee, whether from the church or an indirect arrangement with another organization related to the church, must be included. (See page 164 for a chart of common items of compensation and benefits used in churches and their tax consequences.) In determining reasonable compensation, it does not matter if a benefit is taxable or nontaxable.

> **ELAINE'S EXTRA**
>
> Take care for any employee considered a "disqualified person" under IRC Section 4958. Attention to documentation of benefits is critical for any disqualified person under IRC Section 4958 to avoid creating an automatic excess benefit transaction. See Chapter 2.

Excluded Benefits

Certain economic benefits are disregarded in the analysis of compensation. These include:

- Nontaxable fringe benefits described in IRC Section 132 (see Chapter 9 for a discussion on Section 132 fringe benefits); and

- Amounts paid under an accountable reimbursement plan.

Establish a Value for Benefits

Whether a benefit is a cash benefit or a noncash benefit, it has a value. Even if a benefit is dif-

---

[4] Treas. Reg. Section 53.4958-4(b)(ii)(B)

ficult to value, it needs to be valued at fair market value. The value of the benefit is not based on what the church *may* pay for the benefit.

When a church determines the fair market value of all noncash benefits and adds them to the rest of the individual's compensation, the total needs to fit under the umbrella of reasonable compensation. If not, then something in the package must be eliminated in order to meet IRS requirements.

ELAINE'S EXTRA

The most commonly overlooked items in a compensation package are the benefits provided through tax-favored plans. Examples include the value of health insurance or a benefit received through a special group plan, such as tuition assistance. The key is to review every item that benefits an employee, despite the item's tax treatment or whether or not it is part of a group plan provided to other employees.

Document the Compensation Package

After identifying the benefits and valuing them, appropriately document the compensation package. Churches have different ways to document compensation packages, but the documentation should at least state the decision made by a properly authorized group or person, and it should contain written documents demonstrating what was used in the process to reach that decision. For pastors and senior-level leaders—those considered to be at the executive level of the church's leadership—documentation is most commonly recorded in the meeting minutes of the governing body that approves the compensation. For non-executive level employees, the governing body frequently delegates the compensation authorization to an executive operating within an approved compensation policy and budget. Written minutes or other documentation help show that each benefit provided is in consideration for the performance of services.

All documentation should be kept in the church's custody and securely stored. Individual personnel files should contain summaries of each person's documented compensation package.

Example of Compensation Documentation

First Church's personnel committee is reviewing compensation for the upcoming year. After consulting several salary surveys, the committee determines that reasonable compensation for the senior pastor is $150,000.

The committee then compiles the details of the senior pastor's compensation:

Cash Salary	$80,000
Housing Allowance	$35,000
Medical Insurance	$12,000
403(b) Contribution	$5,000
Youth Camp for Two Children	$500
Life Insurance Policy	$2,000
Disability Policy	$800
Tuition Assistance Plan	$3,000
Auto Allowance	$2,000
Discount at the Church-Related School	$4,000
Travel Expenses for Spouse (to attend a conference together)	$1,500
Total Value of Compensation Package	$145,800
Umbrella of Reasonable Compensation	**$150,000**

The above compensation package completely fits under the umbrella of reasonable compensation. There is only $4,200 left in the overall value available for any other benefits and/or bonuses that may occur during the year. The committee will document the above package in the minutes of its meeting. The tax treatment of each component will be determined by the church's accounting department to assure proper reporting on the pastor's Form W-2.

Although time-consuming, determining reasonable compensation is important. If an IRS examination occurs, the IRS' determination is presumed correct and the burden of proving the reasonableness of compensation is on the church.[5] However, when a church follows the three basic steps of the rebuttable presumption (discussed in Chapter 2) and the steps above, this reverses the situation, placing the burden of proving the compensation is unreasonable on the IRS.

---

[5] Hendriks Furniture. Inc.., TC Memo 1988-133

CHAPTER 3 KEY POINTS:

■ Obtain outside data and perform a thorough analysis to determine reasonable compensation.

■ Identify and value all benefits provided to an employee—both cash and noncash benefits.

■ Document all parts of the compensation package for senior pastors and senior-level staff, and ideally for every compensated employee on the church's staff.

CLASSIFYING WORKERS

What the IRS requires for defining worker classification

Few areas of compensation and payroll receive as much attention from the Internal Revenue Service as worker classification. And few areas of compensation and payroll result in the extensive costs for making mistakes as worker classification.

This chapter discusses the IRS perspective of this topic and how to navigate classifying workers and the proper treatment of independent contractors. The US Department of Labor perspective regarding this subject is addressed in Chapter 5, and Chapter 6 addresses ministerial classifications. Together, these chapters build the framework every church needs to properly handle the highly scrutinized world of worker classifications.

Types of Church Workers

According to the IRS, a church can have four categories of workers:

- Volunteers – workers receiving no compensation

- Ministers – workers meeting certain criteria

- Employees – workers meeting a common law analysis or statutorily defined by the Internal Revenue Code

- Independent Contractors – workers meeting the common law analysis or statutorily defined by the IRC

Common Classification Errors

The classification of workers affects payroll taxes and various fringe benefit plans, and mistakes in classification are costly. Churches regularly make many classification errors due to faulty logic that often sounds like the following:

- "The church has always classified a worker as a contractor, so it must be right."

- "The worker will only be here for a few hours, days, weeks, etc., so it is not worth the effort to set him or her up as an employee."

- "The church does not want employees, so all the workers will be independent contractors."

- "The worker is working from home, so he or she must be an independent contractor."

- "The worker uses 'independent contractor' to describe himself or herself."

- "The biggest church in town treats a group of workers as independent contractors."

- "During an initial trial time, the worker will be an independent contractor. Then, if it works out, he or she will be classified as an employee."

- "The worker is not legally allowed to work in the country, so the church must treat him or her as an independent contractor."

- "The church will pay the worker only once, so it will not matter how the worker is classified."

Unfortunately, this type of thinking leads to faulty decision making affecting churches of all sizes.

Employee or Independent Contractor

In early years, the United States Supreme Court established a five-part test, known as the "Economic Reality Test"[1] for evaluating worker classification. Then for many years, the IRS considered a 20-point test to determine the classification of workers. However, with pressure from Congress, the IRS consolidated the test into 11 primary factors and grouped the factors into 3 groups of consideration: behavioral control, financial control, and the relationship of the parties.[2] Today, this test provides the platform for worker classification analysis.

Behavioral Control

Behavioral factors to help determine if a worker is an employee are:

1. *Instructions the organization gives the worker.* An employee is generally subject to the organization's instruction about when, where, and how to work.

---

[1] United States v. Silk, 331 U.S. 704 (1947)
[2] https://www.irs.gov/pub/irs-pdf/p1779.pdf

For example, the organization will typically instruct employees on:

    (a) when and where to do the task;

    (b) what tools or equipment to use;

    (c) what workers to hire or assist with accomplishing the task;

    (d) where to purchase supplies and services;

    (e) what task must be performed by a specified individual; and

    (f) what order or sequence must be followed in accomplishing the task.

> **ELAINE'S EXTRA**
> The more professional or skilled the position, the less instruction is needed to still meet the behavioral control test.

2. *Training the organization gives the worker.* Specific training to perform a job that is provided by the employer indicates the worker is an employee. A worker obtaining his or her own training—to achieve a proficiency in a certain work area—might indicate the person is an independent contractor.

Example 4-1

First Church hires a counselor. The counselor is a licensed professional and has great latitude in the methodology used in counseling people. First Church determines the counseling practice's hours and requires all counseling to be done at the church offices. Any supplies or equipment are ordered through the church's purchase systems. First Church restricts the counseling to biblically based programs and does not allow any counseling not aligned with its beliefs. First Church also requires the counselor to attend an annual denominational conference designed for counselors working within First Church's denomination. Therefore, First Church maintains behavioral control over the counselor.

Example 4-2

Second Church desires to have access to a counselor as a resource for its members, but it does not want to add an additional department. An arrangement is made with a local counselor to provide services to church members as selected by the church. Second Church arranges the appointments within the schedule of the counselor. Appointments are conducted at the counselor's office, near the church. The counselor operates a full-time practice and sees other clients besides the church's. The counselor may decline to meet with any client sent by the church. Therefore, Second Church does not maintain behavioral control over the counselor.

The more an employer controls what is done and the way it is done, and binds a worker to the policies and processes of the employer, the more likely the behavioral control tests are met. If the behavioral control tests are met, the more likely the worker is an employee.

Financial Control

Financial factors to help determine if a worker is an employee are:

1. *The worker is reimbursed business expenses.* Employers normally cover ordinary and necessary expenses for an employee to perform his or her job. An independent contractor generally bears ordinary and necessary expenses as a part of conducting his or her own business.

2. *The worker's investment.* A worker's investment may vary from electronics to facilities. Employees generally look to employers to make the investment in work-related items, while an independent contractor will generally provide his or her own items.

3. *The availability of the worker's services.* Independent contractors seek and pursue other business opportunities to expand a business base and often do so through advertising, social media, and so on. When a worker does this on behalf of an employer, it is generally an indication that the worker is an employee.

4. *Payment for services.* Employees are generally guaranteed payment of a regular wage for a certain period worked (i.e., hours worked or time devoted to the business). Independent contractors are usually paid by the job. However, in some professions, an hourly rate might be used but the payment is given as certain work is accomplished.

5. *Potential for profit or loss.* An employee is generally given a guaranteed wage and provided with tools and training to perform a specified job. An employee's basic reward for work is not dependent on cost overruns or the timing of payments. An employee does not have the potential to benefit from the profit of the business or bear the burden of the loss from the business (outside of potential bonus structures present in some employment relationships).

Example 4-3

First Church's counselor is subject to the church's accountable expense reimbursement plan for any out-of-pocket expenses for the counseling program. The church provides an office and any furniture and equipment for the program. The counselor is paid a set salary, regardless of the income generated by the program. First Church has financial control of the counselor.

Example 4-4

Second Church enters into a financial arrangement with its counselor to pay for all the sessions conducted with its members at a set hourly rate. Each month, the counselor sends the church a bill for hours spent on the church's members during the month. The counselor bears all the expenses of his or her practice and receives no other financial support from the church. Second Church does not have financial control of the counselor.

The more financial risk borne by the church, the greater financial control is gained by the church. Evaluating risk and reward is the crux of the analysis. The more financial control a church has, the more likely the worker is an employee.

Type of Relationship

Factors to help determine if a worker is an employee are:

1. *Written contracts.* Written contracts define the duties and responsibilities between the parties. While a contract may detail the understanding of the parties to be that of an independent contractor arrangement, it is one of the least important factors in the overall analysis.

2. *Employee benefits.* Providing benefits, such as insurance, pension, vacation, sick time, and/or other benefits generally associated with employment, indicates the worker is an employee.

3. *Length of time work is expected.* An indefinite relationship indicates a worker is an employee. Independent contractors are usually engaged for a specific project or period of time.

4. *If the service provided is integral to the business of the organization.* A worker providing key aspects of an employer's business services is more likely to be controlled by the employer and is more likely to be an employee.

Example 4-5
First Church's counselor has an employment contract detailing the arrangements of the work relationship. The employment contract is for one year, with a new contract to be negotiated at the end of the year. The counseling program is growing, and it is important an employee operate it. Both the counselor and the church expect the counselor to be treated as an employee.

Example 4-6
Second Church contracts with the counselor to define the engagement. The contract is for one year and details the expectations of the church and the counselor. It also defines the hourly rate charged by the counselor. The counselor completed a Form W-9, Request for Taxpayer Identification Number and Certification, for the church so that the church can provide information for the counselor's Form 1099-MISC at the end of the year. The expectation of both the church and the counselor is that they have an independent contractor arrangement.

The presence of a contract, and its terms, helps determine the type of relationship involved and helps reveal whether a worker is an employee. Again, all of this depends on the parameters set by the contract's language and the expectations both parties develop regarding the relationship as a result of that language.

Weighing the Three Groups

No single factor from these three groups is conclusive in the analysis, but certain factors carry more weight than others. Of the three general areas of consideration, behavioral control is given the greatest weight, followed by financial control. The relationship of the parties is granted the least consideration, since the classification of a worker cannot be overcome simply by declaring a worker is an independent contractor.[3]

The examples above show how the factors may be applied and show the differences in the analysis. When using the tests, First Church's counselor is an employee and Second Church's counselor is an independent contractor.

Decision Making Alternatives

Let the IRS Decide

When the church or the worker wants a formal opinion about classification, either may request the IRS to review an arrangement and determine if the worker is an employee or an independent contractor. To do this, either side can fill out Form SS-8, Determination of Worker Status for Purposes of Federal Employment Taxes and Income Tax Withholding. Traditionally, the IRS leans toward employee classification, so the form is less likely to be used by employers. If the form is utilized by a worker disputing his or her classification as an independent contractor, the IRS will contact the employer to gain additional facts.

Section 530 Defense

When there is a long-standing practice of classifying a worker as an independent contractor, even when the analysis proves a contrary determination, Section 530 of the Revenue Act of 1978 provides relief from an employer's share of employment taxes and related penalties. The Section 530 defense, though technical and not used frequently, generally is raised during an employment tax exam where reclassification is proposed by the IRS.

For this defense, special consideration may be granted when an employer has:

- Consistently treated the worker, or all workers in similar positions, as independent contractors for any time after 1978;

- Filed all required Forms 1099-MISC; and

---

[3] Treas. Reg. Section 31.3121(d)-1(a)(3)

- Has a reasonable basis for treating the workers as independent contractors.

While legislative history encourages the Section 530 defense to be "construed liberally in favor of taxpayers,"[4] the Section 530 defense should not be invoked without an in-depth analysis performed by a knowledgeable tax practitioner.

Independent Contractors

If a worker is truly an independent contractor, then the church must create policies and procedures to meet the documentation and reporting requirements of the IRS for the classification.

Documentation

Outside of the "big-box" vendors, i.e., large chain contractors or stores, which are the obvious outside vendors who require no form of annual reporting, transactions with smaller vendors and independent contractors should follow a set pattern:

1. *Document the arrangement.* Use documentation to formalize the arrangement to clarify what work is to be performed, how payments are to be made, and what expenses will be covered by the church.

2. *Determine workers' compensation coverage.* Insurance companies providing workers' compensation coverage for a church may require independent contractors be included in a church's annual calculation. If a contractor carries on her own worker's compensation coverage, a church should obtain proof of the coverage and retain the proof in the church's files.

> **ELAINE'S EXTRA**
> LLC stands for limited liability company. Payments to an LLC are not payments to a corporation and must be reported on the Form 1099-Misc unless the Form W-9 indicates the LLC is taxed as a corporation.

3. *Obtain Form W-9, Request for Taxpayer Identification Number and Certification.* All contractors and vendors, except for the big-box vendors, should complete a Form W-9 prior to being paid. This is a critical step—it should not be postponed. If vendors want payment, they should provide the Form W-9 prior to receiving payment. Once payment is made, an employer has no leverage to obtain information to report payments on Form 1099-MISC at the end of the year. Don't make the mistake of issuing payments while believing the information will not be needed or that it can be obtained at the end of the year. Form W-9 provides

---

[4] "Present Law and Background Relating to Worker Classification for Federal Tax Purposes by the Staff of the Joint Committee on Taxation," May 7, 2007

information establishing the proper name, address, and identifying number of the vendor, and the type of vendor (i.e., sole proprietorship, LLC, partnership or corporation), to determine if the payments must be reported on Form 1099-MISC. If a vendor refuses to provide a completed Form W-9, payments to the vendor are subject to backup withholding of federal income tax at 24percent.

4. *Correctly establish the independent contractor in an accounting system.* All accounting systems have unique ways to tag or notate payments to independent contractors. To correctly report payments to the contractors, these indicators must be set up in the accounting system. For example, a vendor may be set up in the accounting system, but it is necessary to check a box to tell the system the vendor is subject to reporting on Form 1099-MISC.

In addition to tagging the vendor for Form 1099-MISC reporting, some accounting systems will only look to certain accounts to pick up payments to create the Form 1099-MISC. Some payments to vendors for merchandise or parts aren't reported on Form 1099-MISC, so payments must be split and posted to multiple accounts to properly report on Form 1099-MISC.

Example 4-7
First Church's bookkeeper sets up Joe's Plumbing Services as a vendor in the church's accounting system. During the setup, the bookkeeper fails to check the box indicating Joe's Plumbing Services is a "Form 1099-MISC Vendor." At the end of the year, the accounting system issues a report showing the bookkeeper which vendors should receive Form 1099-MISC. Because the indicator box was not checked, Joe's Pluming is not on the list and no Form 1099-MISC is issued.

Classification Errors and Avenues of Correction

Since classification errors occur regularly, churches must become familiar with the options they can use to correct those errors—as well as the potential risks they run if they ignore classification errors.

IRS Voluntary Classification Settlement Program

The IRS, recognizing the prevalence of classification errors by employers, created a voluntary classification settlement program to allow employers to make corrections and move forward in compliance with the rules.

Qualifying employers (qualifications listed below) may reclassify workers from "independent contractors" to "employees" on a prospective basis by paying a small "settlement" fee as opposed to three years' worth of taxes. This closes the door on any future challenges of past classification errors.

Employers qualifying for the program must:

- Presently treat the worker as an independent contractor and have consistently done so over the term of the working relationship;

- Have filed Forms 1099-MISC, as required, for the prior three calendar years; and

- Not be the subject of an IRS payroll tax examination, a DOL examination, or a state payroll examination.

Procedures for program:

- Select the date for the reclassification to begin. It must be the first day of a calendar quarter (i.e., January 1, April 1, July 1, or October 1).

- File Form 8952, Application for Voluntary Classification Settlement Program, at least 60 days prior to the selected reclassification date.

- The Form 8952 calculates the amount due to the IRS, but the amount is not paid until the settlement process is completed.

- The IRS will contact the employer regarding its acceptance or denial of the Form 8952 and issue the proper settlement agreement, if accepted into the program.

> **ELAINE'S EXTRA**
>
> The Voluntary Reclassification Program provides relief from the IRS for the consequences of misclassifying a worker, but the employer may still face consequences from the Department of Labor or state authorities.

If the voluntary classification program is not utilized and the employer opts to reclassify a worker for all future payments, then the employer's risk is associated with the three open tax years prior to the reclassification.

Voluntary Correction When the IRS Program Doesn't Apply

When an employer cannot or does not utilize the Voluntary Classification Program offered by the IRS, the cost of reclassification rises. IRS Publication 4341 provides information regarding the process for filing the correct forms for an employee reclassified from independent contractor to employee. Special tax rates apply in these cases of correction.

The costs of reclassification are:

- When Forms 1099-MISC are filed appropriately for the worker, the total tax assessed is 10.68 percent consisting of

  (1) for the employee, a total of 3.03 percent consisting of;
      (a) Social Security = 1.24 percent;
      (b) Medicare = 0.29 percent; and
      (c) federal income tax = 1.5 percent; plus
  (2) the employer's 7.65 percent portion for Social Security and Medicare.[5]

- When Forms 1099-MISC are not filed for the worker, the total tax assessed is 13.71 percent consisting of

  (1) for the employee, a total of 6.06 percent;
      (a) Social Security = 2.48 percent;
      (b) Medicare = .58 percent, and
      (c) federal income tax = 3 percent; plus
  (2) the employer's 7.65 percent portion for Social Security and Medicare.[6]

The costs to reclassify may be assessed for each of the three tax years open under the appropriate statute of limitations. Besides the taxes due, the employer must file the appropriate Forms W-2.

Example 4-8

After attending the Ultimate Financial and Legal Conference™, First Church's business administrator realizes the church's nursery workers are incorrectly treated as independent contractors instead of employees. In determining how to fix the problem, the Finance Committee asks for an analysis of using the voluntary compliance program versus just changing the workers' classifications as of January 1.

A review of the qualifications indicates First Church qualifies for the voluntary compliance program. The total paid to the nursery workers in 2017 was $10,500. If the voluntary compliance program is used, the settlement fee will be $112.14. If the program is not used, the potential costs, assuming similar wages were paid for 2015 through 2017, is $3,300. Not only does the voluntary program result in a significant costs savings, but it closes the door on an IRS challenge for any prior years.

While not always a popular approach, a church's proactive approach to classification errors

---

[5] IRC Section 3509(a)
[6] IRC Section 3509(b)

may result in significant tax savings as well as be accomplished with less consternation than when the IRS forces a change.

Reporting Payments on Form 1099-MISC

Even with the advancements in accounting software, it is still necessary for churches to understand when vendor payments must be reported on Form 1099-MISC. Understanding the requirements assists the finance team in double checking automated systems.

Recipients of Form 1099-MISC

Payments made to individuals (including businesses established as sole proprietorships), partnerships, and LLCs are reported on Form 1099-MISC. While payments to corporations are generally excluded, the exclusion does not apply to payments to incorporated law firms.

Payments Reported

Payments of $600 or more to an independent contractor during a calendar year should be reported on Form 1099-MISC. The following types of payments should not be reported on Form 1099-MISC:

- Payments for merchandise or parts are not reported unless the amounts are combined with payments for services and the amount for services is not separately stated on the invoice provided by the vendor;

- Reimbursements for expenses accounted to the employer using the same documentation standards as an accountable reimbursement plan; or

- Payments made using the employer's credit card.

Due Dates

The Forms 1099-MISC, reporting amounts in Box 7, are due to the recipient and to the IRS by January 31 each year. This is the due date for both paper forms and forms electronically filed. (Forms 1099-MISC reporting amounts in other boxes are due February 28 or March 31, if filing electronically.) If an employer is filing 250 or more Forms 1099-MISC, the forms must be

ELAINE'S EXTRA
Payments to individuals through a church's benevolence program are not payments for services rendered, but instead are nontaxable gifts. These payments are not reported on Form 1099-Misc or in any other manner to the benevolent recipient. However, if the payment is made on behalf of the benevolent recipient to a third party (such as a landlord), the payment may require reporting on a Form 1099-Misc issued to the third party.

electronically filed. (A waiver may be obtained from the IRS if an employer cannot meet the electronic filing requirements.)

Penalties

Penalties[7] apply if Form 1099-MISC is (1) not filed by the due date; (2) filed on paper when required to file electronically; (3) filed with an inaccuracy or no taxpayer identifying number (TIN); or (4) the paper forms filed are not machine readable.

Penalties are:

- $50 per form, if filed correctly within 30 days of the due date, with a maximum penalty of $536,000 per year ($187,500 for small businesses[8]);

- $100 per form, if correctly filed more than 30 days after the due date, but before August 1, with a maximum penalty of $1.6 million per year ($536,000 for small businesses); or

- $260 per form if filed after August 1, or the information return is never filed, with a maximum penalty of $3.2 million per year ($1.07 million for small businesses).

Additional penalties, based on the above schedule, may also be assessed for failure to provide correct statements to the recipients or the payees.[9] However, if failing to provide recipient statements is intentional, a penalty of $350 per statement can be applied without a maximum limit.

Backup Withholding

If a contractor refuses to provide the church with a TIN, or the IRS informs the church that the TIN is incorrect, then the church must administer a backup withholding of 24 percent on the payments.

If a Form 1099-MISC is not sent to a vendor, the IRS assesses the penalty for not timely filing the form, and a 24-percent amount for federal income tax on the amount that should have been reported on the Form 1099-MISC.

ELAINE'S EXTRA
Normally, the threat of withholding 24 percent of the payment for income taxes will convince a worker to provide the right information to the church. That is why it is so important to obtain the Form W-9 prior to making any payments to contractors.

---

[7] IRC Section 6721
[8] A small business is defined as a business whose average annual gross receipts for the 3 most recent tax years ending before the calendar year in which the returns are due are $5 million or less.
[9] IRC Section 6722

Backup withholding is deposited on the church's regular deposit schedule and is reported on Form 945, Annual Return of Withheld Federal Income Tax, each year.

CHAPTER 4 KEY POINTS:

- Common worker classification errors must be avoided.

- Worker classification is determined by a thoughtful analysis of the facts and circumstances surrounding the employment arrangement.

- If errors in worker classification are made, there are ways to correct them.

- Proper classification, documentation, and reporting is crucial to avoid and reduce the financial risks errors pose to the church.

FLSA WORKER CLASSIFICATION

How a landmark federal law shapes the ways
that ministers and employees are classified

When working on payroll and compensation, churches need to understand the basics of employee classification for wage and hour rules. This type of classification is not subject to Internal Revenue Service (IRS) oversight, but is subject to US Department of Labor (DOL) oversight. As a category, DOL employee classifications ranks near the top of the list of violations most commonly made by churches. Churches must understand the basic framework of wage and hour rules to avoid errors caused by common misconceptions, bad habits, and lack of knowledge.[1]

This chapter is a primer on the subject of wage and hour laws. It does not cover all the nuances and complications that arise in a church setting, which are too numerous to cover here. The aim of this chapter is to alert churches to general principles so that leaders will be aware of the need to consult with professionals—and know the right questions to ask those professionals.

History of the FLSA

The Fair Labor Standards Act (FLSA), signed into law in 1938 by President Franklin D. Roosevelt, banned most child labor, established a minimum wage of 25 cents an hour, created a 44-hour work week, and set a salary test for exempt positions at $100 per week. Today, the FLSA establishes a minimum wage of $7.25 an hour, maintains a 40-hour work week, and sets

---

[1] Before making any decisions about the application of the FLSA, churches should consult with an employment lawyer or human resources professional: https://www.dol.gov/whd/overtime/fs17a_overview.htm

a salary test for exempt positions at $455 per week.

Many commentators propose that the FLSA does not apply to churches. That may have once been true, but the church of today is not the church of yesterday. Advanced activities easily make the law applicable to most churches, either on an entity level (meaning the FLSA applies to the church operations as a whole) or on an individual employee basis based on the employee's duties. Given the two ways the FLSA may apply in a church setting, no church should assume the FLSA does not apply to it or to any of its employees.

Warning: *Besides federal requirements, every state maintains its own version of the FLSA, either layering additional rules on top of federal rules or applying similar rules where the federal rules don't apply. The law most favorable to an employee, whether at the state or federal level, always applies.*

Worker Classifications

Under the FLSA and DOL rules, there are three primary classifications for church employees:

- Employees meeting the "ministerial exception"

- Exempt employees

- Nonexempt employees

ELAINE'S EXTRA

Job descriptions for all employees are important, but especially for those whose work qualifies for the ministerial exception. Employee classifications, and the wage implications related to them, may be won or lost based on job descriptions.

The Ministerial Exception

Established more through judicial application of the law than through any statute, employment law embraces a concept known as the "ministerial exception." The concept revolves around the idea that government does not have authority to intervene in the relationship between a church and its ministers. Matters between a church and its ministers, including salary, are of ecclesiastical concern only,[2] and any governmental intervention violates the First Amendment protections guaranteeing separation of church and state. When an employee qualifies for the "ministerial exception," it means the FLSA cannot apply to that employee with respect to his or her employment relationship with the church.[3]

---

[2] McClure v. Salvation Army, 460 F.2d 553 (5th Cir. 1972).

[3] The ministerial exception also applies to other areas of employment law.

Who qualifies as a "minister" for this exception is different from who qualifies as a "minister" for other payroll tax rules enforced by the IRS (discussed in Chapter 6). For employment law, to be considered a minister, an employee must perform essential religious duties as a required element of the employee's job that cannot be avoided, ignored, or delegated without employer recourse.[4] Unlike the concept of "minister" for the Internal Revenue Code, the employee is not required to have ministerial credentials. Without this requirement, the group of employees eligible for the ministerial exception is wider for DOL classification purposes.

A position qualifying an employee for the ministerial exception may include:

- A requirement of previous religious training or ongoing religious training, such as continuing education requirements;

- A title reflecting spiritual or religious duties or a spiritual position;

- Duties supporting and/or conveying the core beliefs of the church;

- Duties of conveying the message and teachings of the church;

- Selecting or creating the religious content for a program; and/or

- Leading others to grow or mature in their faith.

The first step in working with classifications and the FLSA is identifying employees that meet the "ministerial exception."

Example 5-1

Suzy is the director of children's ministry at First Church. She selects the curriculum and leads all the children's ministry workers in learning the curriculum and preparing for their teaching duties. She also leads children's church each Sunday morning and Wednesday evening. Suzy is not a licensed or ordained minister of the gospel and does not qualify to be treated as a minister for federal tax purposes. A review of Suzy's duties and position indicates she performs essential religious duties and qualifies for the ministerial exception. Suzy is not subject to the FLSA wage and hour rules.

Exempt Employees

After reviewing the duties of employees and identifying those who qualify for the ministerial exception, the next step is to categorize the remaining employees either as exempt or nonexempt. Start by determining which employees are exempt before evaluating which ones are nonexempt.[5]

---

[4] Hosanna-Tabor Evangelical Lutheran Church and School v. E.E.O.C., 565 U.S. 171 (2012).

[5] www.flsa.com/coverage.html

Salary Test. An exempt employee's compensation must be at least $455 per week and paid on a salaried basis. This is a minimum salary amount. It is not prorated for employees working part time. An employee that does not receive the minimum salary amount cannot be an exempt employee.

A "salaried basis" means the salary is the same rate if paid every week, regardless of the number of hours worked. The employer may not dock the employee's pay in less than one-day increments for disciplinary reasons. The employer may track paid time off in any time increment.[6]

Example 5-2

George is a church business administrator. His duties include extensive authority over the business administration of the church, and he directly supervises 10 employees. George's compensation is $400 per week. At his compensation rate, George cannot be classified as an exempt employee. George is a nonexempt employee and is subject to the FLSA wage and hour rules. Even though George's duties may meet one of the duties' tests for exempt employees, his duties are never evaluated because he receives less than the $455 per week minimum to qualify as an exempt employee.

If an employee passes the salary test, then the employee is evaluated based on his or her duties.

Duties Test. To be considered exempt, an employee's duties must be described in one of four major classifications set by the DOL for determining exempt status. Employees meet one of these classifications, and thus become classified as exempt, when at least 80 percent of their time is spent on the classification's duties and responsibilities. The four classifications are:

I. Executive Exemption: Manages the organization, or a distinct department, supervising at least two full-time employees (these individuals cannot be volunteers), and possessing the authority to hire and fire employees.

II. Administrative Exemption: Office work or non-manual labor relating to the management of the organization, exercising significant discretion and independent judgement on matters of sig-

> **ELAINE'S EXTRA**
> Administrative assistants rarely have the discretion and the authority in the church to meet the administrative exemption qualification. As such, most administrative assistants, even the senior pastor's assistant, do not qualify as exempt employees.

---

[6] The salary test is more complicated than this summary. Churches should check the DOL website for more details. https://www.dol.gov/whd/overtime/fs17g_salary.pdf

nificance. These employees may have significant leadership roles, but do not have the staff reporting to them to meet the executive exemption. Leadership roles also may be fulfilled by administering an area where volunteer labor is a significant factor in carrying out the programs. Employees should have significant abilities to operate in a manner of authority over an area or a program.

III. Professional Exemption: Employees with a high level of training and a special skill set. Examples include attorneys, teachers (but not daycare workers), engineers, and accountants/CPAs.

IV. Computer Professional: This group includes systems analysts, programmers, and software engineers. This group does not include network administrators or other general IT employees.

Warning: *"Exempt employee" and "salaried employee" are not synonymous terms. The existence of an equalized and consistent pay arrangement does not determine if an employee is an exempt employee or a nonexempt employee. A salaried employee is paid a consistent amount each pay period, but the employee still may be classified as a nonexempt employee if the weekly pay is under $455 or the employee does not meet one of the "duties" tests.*

Nonexempt Employees

With both the "ministerial exception" and exempt classifications addressed, the final step is to classify all remaining church employees as nonexempt employees. Nonexempt employees usually constitute the majority of a church's workforce. This group is subject to minimum wage requirements and overtime pay for all hours worked exceeding 40 hours in the work week.

Warning: *State laws must be researched. Some states reduce the required number of hours an employee needs to work before receiving overtime pay. Some states may even apply overtime based on the number of hours an employee works per day. These examples underscore the reason churches must become familiar with state laws. Remember, the law most favorable to an employee applies.*

Work Week

A work week is defined by the FLSA as any 7-day period selected by the employer. For federal purposes, a nonexempt employee who actually works more than 40 hours during this 7-day period must be paid overtime for all hours worked beyond 40 hours at the rate of time and one-half the employee's regular pay rate. Stated another way, hours paid for nonwork time, such as paid vacation time, do not count towards the 40 hours worked to determine overtime hours.

Example 5-3

Joe works in the maintenance department of the church as a nonexempt employee. For the week of July 4, Joe's timecard shows 45 hours. His paid time off for July 4 represents 8 hours, which is subtracted from the 45 hours total. That leaves 37 hours of time actually worked during the work week. Hence, Joe's actual work hours are less than 40 in total, so no overtime pay is owed. Joe should be paid his regular rate of pay for all 45 hours.

Example 5-4

Same facts as Example 5-3, except Joe's timecard instead shows 50 hours of work time. The 8 hours attributable to the holiday again are subtracted, but this time from the 50-hour total. That leaves 42 hours of time actually worked, which means Joe is owed 2 hours of overtime pay and 48 hours at his regular rate of pay.

Warning: *Overtime is paid in increments of 6 minutes per federal statute. Overtime is also due to an employee whether or not the overtime has been authorized by the appropriate supervisor. Churches should be aware of potential overtime causes in order to appropriately budget for the additional payroll costs.*

ELAINE'S EXTRA

Most churches are surprised by the DOL's recordkeeping requirements and even more surprised to learn that the DOL will be more willing to take the word of an employee over the word of the employer when determining hours worked where recordkeeping is lacking.

Recordkeeping

Employers are responsible for creating and enforcing, accurate recordkeeping systems to capture the hours nonexempt employees work. Accurate recordkeeping systems will require an employee to indicate the time work started and the time work ended. This includes "clocking in and out" for nonwork hours during the day, such as the lunch hour. If an employee continues to work through their lunch time, they must be paid for this time even if the additional work time is not requested by a supervisor.

Warning: *State employment law dictates the minimum of and length of breaks that are required to be provided to nonexempt employees.*

Recordkeeping of hours worked is required for all nonexempt employees, even if the pay arrangement is a salary arrangement for a set amount each week and the amount of hours worked does not vary each week. Recordkeeping proves the amount paid for the hours worked at least equals the minimum wage, and any overtime hours have been compensated at the proper overtime rate.

Common Myths and Errors Churches Make Regarding Nonexempt Employees

Compensatory Time between Weeks

Both employees and churches often misunderstand compensatory time. It is a common myth that compensatory time or "comp time" allows for time off in one work week based on over-time hours worked in a different work week. The DOL only allows compensatory time within the same work week as the additional hours are worked. Each work week must stand on its own in regards to overtime calculations.

> **ELAINE'S EXTRA**
>
> Most "myths," such as comp time, are perpetuated because many "other" churches follow them, or "large" churches follow them. It's good to remember that the common practices of the majority, or of large churches, can still be wrong.

Example 5-5
Betty is First Church's full-time financial secre-tary. Getting ready for the finance team's upcom-ing budget meeting, Betty works 52 hours in one week. Instead of paying Betty overtime rate for 12 hours, the church tells her she can take the 12 hours off the next week. This is a prohib-ited arrangement, since the time off occurs in a different work week from the one in which the overtime occurred.

Nonexempt Employees that Volunteer

Nonexempt employees may love the area of the church which employs them and have a natural desire to "volunteer" in the same area. However, nonexempt employees shouldn't be allowed to volunteer in the same area in which they work. The DOL's position is that volunteer time in the same area as employment is extended job time and is compensable time.[7]

Example 5-6
Nancy is the youth department's administrative assistant. She loves young people and wants to volunteer as a chaperone at youth events. Due to her position, Nancy should not be allowed to volunteer as a chaperone, since it may not be possible to determine when she is performing volunteer activities versus employment activities.

Accidental Work Time

Churches require a lot of "accidental" work time from nonexempt employees. The minister

---

7 http://webapps.dol.gov/elaws/whd/flsa/docs/publicvol.asp

who consistently texts his or her assistant after hours or on weekends creates accidental work time. Another staff or church member who asks a staff member to perform a task on Sunday morning or Wednesday evening creates hours worked. Ministers and other administrators must be trained to respect the boundaries of the work hours with nonexempt employees to avoid creating accidental work hours. Any employee instructed to always respond to the text or the call is technically placed on an "on-call" basis, and the church must compensate the employee for 24 hours a day.

Example 5-7

Kelly is the senior pastor's administrative assistant. She is an excellent assistant and always responds to any request from the pastor, no matter the time or the day. Unfortunately, the pastor works without regard to the clock and often texts or calls Kelly during the evenings or the weekends. Kelly never records this time on her timecard. The pastor is creating accidental work time for Kelly, and Kelly must be compensated for this time.

Warning: *Another common way churches create "accidental work time" is to require employees to attend church services or other church events. Any time an employee is "required" to be someplace to meet a job requirement, the church is required to pay them for the time.*

Timekeeping for Salaried Nonexempt Employees

Churches love salary arrangements because they allow for predictable budgeting and fixed operating costs. The myth is that all salaried employees are exempt employees and no timekeeping records are required. The simple establishment of a flat or "salaried" wage does not qualify an employee as automatically exempt from overtime. It is possible to pay a nonexempt employee a salary, but records must exist proving the time this employee worked each week.

Example 5-8

Kelly, the senior pastor's administrative assistant, normally works 35 hours per week and is paid $400 per week for all hours worked up to 40 hours per week. Kelly must turn in time records to prove (1) the weeks when she does not work more than 40 hours and (2) the weeks when she works more than 40 hours and must receive overtime pay.

Failure to maintain time records for any nonexempt employee leaves the church vulnerable to a DOL wage assessment. When the employer cannot provide proof of time worked, the DOL will look to the employee to provide a schedule of hours worked.

CHAPTER 5 KEY POINTS:

- Churches are not automatically exempt from the Fair Labor Standards Act.

- Churches must review all employees and classify them into one of three categories: (1) "ministerial," (2) "exempt," or (3) "nonexempt."

- Most church employees are classified as nonexempt and timekeeping systems are mandatory, even if the employee is paid on a "salary" basis.

MINISTERS & THE PAYROLL PROCESS

Applying special rules consistently for qualifying ministers

Ministers enjoy special rules for federal income tax, Social Security tax, Medicare tax, and several popular benefits, but navigating payroll issues for ministers is complicated. Following tax rules correctly (or incorrectly) immediately affects a church's payroll tax obligations. That's why understanding tax rules for ministers' payroll is so important.

Who Is a Minister

When working on payroll, a church must first determine which employees are ministers for federal tax purposes to see if the special rules for ministers need to be applied. Federal tax law doesn't define "minister of the gospel."[1] Lacking a clear legislative definition of a minister, the courts have wrestled with the overall application of who is treated as a minister for federal tax law. There is some guidance from the courts, though, and the determination involves two areas of identification and analysis.

1. Credentials

Providing for latitude in differences, not only between religious bodies, but also within a religious body, Congress provides a multiple-word reference to credentials using "duly ordained, commissioned, or licensed minister."[2]

Variations in the rights and privileges of ministers within a religious body may exist, but to be classified as a minister for federal tax purposes, a minister must have something that sets him

---

[1] IRC Section 107
[2] IRC Section 1402(c)(4)

or her apart as a minister, and that "something" must be granted to the minister by a church.[3]

Because churches do use a variety of terms in granting credentials to persons in the ministry, the courts have provided further guidance on what sets a minister apart from other positions by interpreting the meaning of a "duly ordained, commissioned, or licensed minister." This guidance is used by churches, professionals, and the courts when a variation in the rights conferred by churches brings the determination into question. The Tax Court, in the *Knight v. Commissioner*[4] decision, clarified a balancing test of five factors to be used:

1. Administration of the sacraments;

2. Conducting religious worship;

3. Having management responsibility in a local church or denomination;

4. Ordained, commissioned, or licensed; and

5. Considered a religious leader by one's church or denomination.[5]

The fourth factor is a requisite factor in all ministerial determinations. The remaining four factors are balanced. The more factors met, the stronger the case is for minister classification. Churches must make this full analysis for all staff members with ministerial credentials from a church to determine which ones qualify to receive the full rights of a minister.

Example 6-1

Joe is a commissioned minister of First Church. First Church both commissions and ordains ministers. As a commissioned minister, Joe may not administer the sacraments, perform marriages, or participate in the church's governance decisions. He is authorized to preach and spiritually minister to the members of the congregation. Applying the above tests, Joe conducts religious worship services, he is commissioned, and he is viewed as a spiritual leader of the congregation. Meeting three out of the five factors established by the courts, Joe is a "duly ordained, commissioned, or licensed minister."

Warning: *If an organization isn't qualified as a church, as defined by the IRS,[6] the credentials issued by that organization are not recognized by the IRS as ministerial credentials and do not qualify a person to be a minister.*

---

[3]   Knight v. Commissioner, 92 T.C. 199 (1989)

[4]   Knight, *supra*

[5]   Knight, *supra*

[6]   The church must be classified as a religious organization under IRC Sections 501(c)(3) and 170(b)(1)(A)(i).

2. Duties

For an employee to be classified as a minister for federal tax purposes, the employee must also perform duties applicable to those services performed by a minister in the "exercise of his ministry." Defined by the Treasury Regulations, these include:

- the ministration of sacerdotal functions;

- the conduct of religious worship;

- the control, conduct, and maintenance of religious organizations under the authority of a religious body constituting a church or church denomination;

- the performance of teaching and administrative duties at theological seminaries; and

- services performed under an assignment or designation by a religious body constituting the minister's church.[7]

> **ELAINE'S EXTRA**
>
> The IRS believes sacerdotal duties are limited to weddings, funerals, baptisms, and communion. The definition used by the IRS has not been created by law or regulation. The term "sacerdotal" refers to duties expected to be performed by a minister—it is determined by the church, not by the IRS, and may be broader than the IRS definition.

Application and Analysis by Churches

Churches should apply a two-step process to identify ministers and correctly administer the federal tax laws:

Step 1: Determine and know which employees are "commissioned, licensed, or ordained." Determine this at the beginning of the employment relationship and obtain a copy of the minister's credentials for the personnel files. (If credentials may renew at certain times, update the personnel file as needed.)

Step 2: Review the employee's job description to determine if he or she performs ministerial duties as recognized by the Treasury Regulations and the courts.[8] Maintaining good job descriptions greatly assists in the process. If challenged by the IRS, the job description is the primary support for minister classification. The ministerial duties must be the majority of the duties and not just a small or inconsequential portion of the duties.

Warning: *If an employee works for an organization other than a church, the duties test is more*

---

[7] Treas. Reg. Section 1.1402(c)-5(b)(2)

[8] The IRS believes more than 50 percent of the minister's duties must be "ministerial duties" as defined by the regulations, but this percentage is not stated through any statute or regulation.

restrictive and cannot include duties involving the management responsibilities of the orga-nization.

ELAINE'S EXTRA

Payroll tax laws may apply even if a minister is working for a church that is not his or her credentialing church body or denomination. It is important to identify credentials at the start of the employment relationship.

Conclusion: If an employee passes the tests in Steps 1 and 2, the employee is treated as a minister for federal tax purposes. If the employee fails either the test in Step 1 or Step 2, the employee is not a minister for federal tax purposes.

Example 6-2

Lola is an ordained minister with a love of all things related to media. She takes a position at First Church as a part of its media department. She is not the manager of the department. Lola also teaches a Sunday school class, but this duty is not a part of her job description. Lola meets the test in Step 1, but she does not meet the test in Step 2, since most of her duties are not ministerial duties. Lola may not be treated as a "minister" by First Church for federal tax purposes.

The Minister and Worker Classification

Despite preferential payroll withholding rules (discussed later in this chapter), a church must determine if a minister is an employee or independent contractor. However, due to the nature of the employment relationship, substantial behavioral control doesn't have to exist to classify a minister as an employee. Other factors, such as financial factors, may serve as an indicator of the employee relationship. (A discussion of the factors indicating employee status is in Chapter 4.) When a minister predominantly works for a single church, he is most likely an employee of the church.

ELAINE'S EXTRA

Since ministers are not subject to regular tax and withholding rules, churches may tend to take the easy way out and issue a Form 1099-MISC reporting taxable earnings. But note: any minister receiving a Form 1099-MISC is not eligible for tax-favored health insurance benefits as well as many other tax favored benefits.

As with other workers, the analysis of worker classification determines a minister's proper reporting format (i.e., Form W-2 or Form 1099-MISC) and his qualification for fringe benefits. Most fringe benefit programs are not available for independent contractors. (See Chapters 8, 9, and 10 for further discussions of fringe benefits.)

Example 6-3

Pastor Smith is the only worker at Second Church. He receives a housing allowance, taxable salary, and health insurance. Taking the easy path of reporting, the church's treasurer reports Pastor Smith's taxable earnings on Form 1099-MISC. Because Pastor Smith's income is reported on Form 1099-MISC, the amount the church pays for his health insurance premiums is a taxable benefit.

The Minister and the Church's Payroll Tax Obligations

For employers, the Internal Revenue Code defines payroll tax obligations in two primary areas: (1) federal income tax withholding and (2) Social Security/Medicare tax withholding. The Code determines what income is subject to taxes and the related tax withholding requirements.

Federal Income Tax Withholding

Ministers are exempt from mandatory withholding of federal income taxes from their salary.[9] Ministers can elect that an employer withhold federal income taxes by completing either a Form W-4 or by giving written instructions to the church. The exemption from withholding federal income taxes from a minister's pay should not be construed as an exemption from federal income tax.[10] Without written authorization to withhold federal income tax, a church may not withhold the taxes from the minister's pay. Therefore, it is important that a minister clearly communicate his expectations regarding the payment of federal income taxes.

> **ELAINE'S EXTRA**
>
> Ministers may either pay their income taxes through federal income tax withholding or by making estimated tax payments throughout the year. Either option requires a minister to estimate the total tax for the year to make the right tax payments.

Example 6-4

Pastor Smith works for First Church. At the end of the year, his tax preparer questions why his Form W-2 doesn't have any income tax withholding reported in Box 2. Curious, Pastor Smith asks the payroll department why it has not withheld federal income tax from his taxable pay. The payroll clerk tells him that since he never provided a completed Form W-4 or any other instructions to the church regarding withholding for federal income taxes, the church may not withhold income taxes from his pay.

---

[9]   IRC Section 3401(a)(9)

[10]   In re Pomeroy, KTC 2003-220 (D.Nev. 2003)

Social Security and Medicare Tax Withholding

Non-minister employees pay into the Social Security and Medicare programs through the Federal Insurance Contributions Act (FICA). The FICA/Medicare program requires an employer to withhold one-half of the tax, the employee's contribution, and match the other half of the tax, the employer's contribution. Ministers, performing ministerial duties, **do not and cannot participate** in the FICA program. This is not an elective decision for the minister or the church, but a decision mandated by law.[11]

> **ELAINE'S EXTRA**
>
> Ministers should estimate their self-employment tax and include it with the income tax paid through withholding of federal income tax by the church or in their quarterly estimated tax payments.

Ministers pay into the Social Security system through the Self Employment Contributions Act (SECA.) Ministerial earnings are, as defined by law, self-employment income.[12] The result is that a church is prohibited from withholding and matching Social Security/Medicare taxes for a minister as required for other employees. Ministers report earnings on Schedule SE with the Form 1040 unless they have an approved Form 4361. (The Form 4361 is discussed later in this chapter.)

Example 6-5

Joe serves First Church as the new executive pastor. His duties include overall supervision of the administration of the church, preaching one Sunday each month, and teaching a class each Wednesday night. Joe is ordained by First Church. Joe recently left a corporate job and is new to working in a church. Joe requests the payroll department withhold Social Security and Medicare taxes with employer matching on his taxable pay. Because Joe meets the definition of a minister performing ministerial duties, Joe's request cannot be honored by First Church.

> **ELAINE'S EXTRA**
>
> Many churches voluntarily increase a minister's compensation package by the 7.65 percent the church would pay in FICA/Medicare taxes for a non-minister employee. Often referred to as the SECA Allowance, the amount is a part of a minister's taxable compensation package.

Warning: *When a minister has Social Security and Medicare taxes withheld from paychecks, essentially this is telling the IRS he or she is not a minister for federal tax*

---

[11] IRC Section 3121 (b)(8)
[12] IRC Section 1402(a)(8)

purposes. If not a minister for federal tax purposes, then he or she is not eligible for the housing allowance provided by IRC Section 107. (See Chapter 11 for a discussion of the housing allowance.)

Opting Out of Self-Employment Tax

Until the 1967 amendments to the Social Security Act of 1935, ministers didn't regularly participate in the Social Security program unless they annually elected into the program. The 1967 amendments switched the system, bringing ministers into the Social Security program. As a part of this change, ministers became a part of the Social Security system by having their earnings "from the performance of their ministerial duties" defined to be earnings from self-employment.[13]

Acknowledging that some ministers may have a religious- or conscience-based objection to the government-funded program, the law allows ministers to opt out of the program.[14] Form 4361 (Application for Exemption for Self-Employment Tax for Use by Ministers, Members of Religious Orders and Christian Science Practitioners) is used by a minister to opt out of the self-employment tax on ministerial earnings.[15]

For ministers to be able to claim this exemption from Self-Employment Tax, they must meet the following requirements:

1. The minister must be a duly ordained, commissioned, or licensed minister of a church qualifying as a religious organization under IRC Section 501(c)(3).[16]

2. The minister opposes public insurance based on sincerely held religious beliefs against any public insurance that makes payments in the event of death, disability, old age, or retirement, or that makes payments toward the cost of, or provides services for, medical

ELAINE'S EXTRA

Confusion exists among churches and ministers that if the minister has not opted out of self-employment tax by filing Form 4361, then he or she may elect to have Social Security/Medicare taxes withheld and matched. This is not correct and should not be done.

---

[13] IRC Section 1402(b)(8)
[14] IRC Section 1402(e)
[15] This election is different from the exemption provided to certain religious groups where the members also forfeit all benefits from Social Security. Ministers who elect out of Social Security for their ministerial earnings do not forfeit their Social Security benefits earned from non-ministerial earnings.
[16] Rev. Rul. 76-415, 1976-2 CB 255

care, of which any part of the payments is based on—or measured by—his or her earnings from his or her services in his or her capacity as a minister.[17]

Being opposed to public insurance based on sincerely held religious beliefs does not include beliefs that the Social Security system won't be around when the minister retires or that the minister is a better financial manager than the government. These beliefs may be sincerely held, but they do not qualify as a "religious belief," according to tax law.[18] Ministers must be able to support and defend their beliefs if questioned by any government or judicial authority. If a minister cannot honestly state in court that such a religious belief exists, he or she does not qualify for the exemption.

3. The Form 4361 must be filed, in triplicate, in a timely manner. The key to determining timely filing is the date the minister receives his or her credentials. The due date is calculated based on the date a minister receives his credentials and when he receives his first income from being a minister after receiving his credentials. The form is due by the due date of the minister's tax return, including extensions, for the second year after credentials are obtained, in which there were self-employment earnings of $400 or more (any part of which are from his duties as a minister).[19] This due date is difficult to understand and is best explained through the following example:

Example 6-6
Joe is ordained by First Church in December of 2017 and receives compensation from the church for December totaling $1,250. Joe's due date for filing Form 4361 is the due date of his 2018 Form 1040.

Warning: *The timing requirement begins with the first set of credentials defining a person to be a minister for federal tax purposes. Obtaining new credentials does not restart the two-year period for filing the form.[20] Only in instances when the minister leaves the ministry for a period of time, then enters the ministry of another faith with a new belief system, may the time for filing Form 4361 restart.[21]*

Example 6-7
Sue was licensed by First Church in 2006 and worked as a minister from 2006 through 2017. In 2017, Sue was ordained by First Church and she wants to file Form 4361 to claim the exemption from self-employment tax. Sue cannot file Form 4361 because the due

---

[17] Treas. Reg. Section 1.1402(e)-2A, *and see* Hairston v. Commissioner, T.C. Memo 51,025 (1995)
[18] Rev. Rul. 70-197, 1970-1 CB 181
[19] Vigil v. Commissioner, T.C. Summary Opinion 2008-6 and Bennett v. Commissioner, T.C. Memo 2007-355
[20] Ballinger v. Commissioner, 78 T.C. 752 *affd* 53 AFTR 2d 84-908
[21] Hall v. Commission, 74 AFTR 2d 94-5555

date for filing was triggered in 2006, when she was licensed as a minister by First Church.

The form cannot be filed with—or as an attachment to—a minister's Form 1040. If the Form 4361 is filed in this manner, it will never be approved, and it is not considered as filed for the "timely filing" requirements.

Proof of timely filing may be necessary if the application is lost in the mail or in IRS processing. The form should be mailed "certified return receipt" to provide proof of filing.

4. Ministers filing Form 4361 are required to notify the church or denomination who issued their credentials.

5. The election only applies to ministerial earnings and not to other secular income.[22]

6. The election is not valid until the IRS returns an approved Form 4361 to the minister. Approval is retroactive to the minister's credentialing date. If a minister pays self-employment tax on ministerial earnings while waiting on the form's approval, a refund may be requested by filing Form 1040X, Amended U.S. Individual Income Tax Return.

Example 6-8

Joe (from Example 6-6) timely filed Form 4361 and, if approved, the election will be valid back to Joe's ordination date. But if Joe has not received the approved election by the time he files his 2017 Form 1040, he must pay the self-employment tax with his return.

The approved form can rarely be replaced, so a minister should take precautions to keep copies of the approved form in several locations. If questioned by the IRS, a min-

---

ELAINE'S EXTRA

Some ministers have been able to convince the court to allow them the exemption even when they cannot produce an approved form when they convince the court that the form was properly and timely filed.

ELAINE'S EXTRA

Any minister obtaining the exemption must be prepared to take specific steps to replace any benefits that may be forfeited or significantly reduced by the exemption. Ministers claiming the exemption need to make plans to replace retirement income, disability income, and survivor benefits. Waiting until a minister turns 60 or older is too late to consider the long-term consequences of the exemption.

---

[22] Williams v. Commissioner, T.C. Memo 1999-105

ister must produce an approved Form 4361. Without credible evidence, the IRS may not allow the exemption, and it will assess self-employment tax.[23]

Warning: *The election out of self-employment tax is a personal responsibility. It is not the responsibility of the church to file the form for a minister or to encourage a minister to file the form. For ministers wanting to opt out, they must (1) determine their eligibility, (2) weigh the consequences of opting out, and (3) fill out the form, send it in, and receive the approval in a timely manner. It's very important that ministers understand the consequences of opting out. For a church with a minister who is opting out, the church will treat the minister the same with or without a Form 4361 approval, so the church doesn't need to obtain a copy or verify the exemption as a part of its responsibilities.*

CHAPTER 6 KEY POINTS:

- A church must determine which employees are ministers.

- A minister, performing ministerial duties, may never pay into Social Security and Medicare through the FICA program. He or she must pay self-employment tax on the earnings.

- If a minister desires to opt out of self-employment tax, he or she must take special care to understand the qualifications for the election and follow all steps to timely obtain the election.

- A church's payroll functions are never affected by a minister's decision to opt out of self-employment tax.

---

[23] Fredric A. Gardner, et ux. v. Commissioner, TC Memo 2013-67

NUTS & BOLTS OF THE PAYROLL PROCESS

Blending regulatory and tax compliance with effective payroll systems

Working on a church's payroll requires many decisions and a series of complicated tasks prior to writing the first payroll check. If the number of employees grows, even more decisions are necessary to allow payroll to operate smoothly and in compliance with all the varying regulators. In order to properly do all of this, it's important to become familiar with both federal and state government obligations.

Federal Government Obligations

Federal Registrations

Churches with payroll obligations need to register in two ways with the Internal Revenue Service:

- **Employer Identification Number (EIN).** All businesses, including churches, cannot operate without an EIN, either with or without employees. This identifying number is used for all IRS reporting obligations and with other regulators and banks to identify an entity or business operation. An EIN is obtained by filing Form SS-4, Application for Employer Identification Number, with the IRS. The Form SS-4 may be filed in paper form by either mail or by fax or online.[1]

---

[1] Form SS-4 may be filed online at https://www.irs.gov/businesses/small-businesses-self-employed/apply-for-an-employer-identification-number-ein-online. The paper form can be found at https://www.irs.gov/pub/irs-pdf/fss4.pdf and the instructions are found at https://www.irs.gov/pub/irs-pdf/iss4.pdf.

Note the following EIN precautions:

> **Use only one EIN for the church.** The EIN is assigned to the corporate entity and it covers all activities of the corporate entity. If a church establishes a separate division, but not a separate entity, it should use the same EIN for all church activities.

> **Account for all activities.** Every activity operating under the EIN is a part of the church and should be accounted for as a part of the church's operations. A church should not allow its EIN to be used for any account, banking or otherwise, unless it is taking responsibility for the account and accounting for the activity in the account.

• **Electronic Federal Tax Payment System (EFTPS).** Federal tax payments must be made electronically. If a church is not using a professional service, EFTPS should be used for depositing payroll taxes. Registering with EFTPS will give a church credentials to electronically deposit payroll taxes. As soon as a church obtains an EIN, it should register for EFTPS, because the wait time for receiving registration approval and credentials may take up to two weeks. The EFTPS system is accessed at eftps.gov/eftps.

Note the following EFTPS precautions:

> **Potential penalties.** When tax deposits are required to be submitted through EFTPS, but they are not submitted through the EFTPS system, they are subject to deposit penalties.

> **Account for the required processing time.** Payments through EFTPS may need to be scheduled one or more days in advance of the due date to account for system processing time requirements.

Federal Tax Obligations

Churches must also adhere to tax withholding and payment obligations, which include:

• **Federal Income Tax.** For virtually all non-minister employees, federal income tax must be withheld from cash pay and from certain noncash forms of pay. Withholding is based on taxable income for the pay period utilizing information obtained from the employee's

Form W-4 and the corresponding prescribed tax table issued by the IRS.

- **Social Security Tax.** Social Security tax must be withheld, with limited exceptions, from all non-minister employees, at 6.2 percent, with the employer paying a matching amount of 6.2 percent. Each year, federal law establishes a wage base on which the tax is assessed in the calendar year.

- **Medicare Tax.** Medicare tax must be withheld from all non-minister employees at 1.45 percent (with limited exceptions). The employer pays a matching amount of 1.45 percent. There is no wage base for Medicare tax calculations. The tax is assessed on all taxable wages.

- **Additional Medicare Tax.** For all taxable wages paid over $200,000, an additional Medicare tax of 0.9 percent must be withheld. There is no employer matching for the additional Medicare tax.

- **Federal Unemployment Tax.** Since organizations exempt under IRC Section 501(c)(3) are exempt from federal unemployment tax, this employer-funded tax is not paid by churches.

Churches' Potential Exemptions from Social Security and Medicare Taxes

- **Form 8274.** Churches and church-controlled organizations may elect to opt out of the Social Security and Medicare tax system based on religious beliefs.[2] Churches make the election by filing Form 8274, Certification by Churches and Qualified Church-Controlled Organizations Electing Exemption from Employer Social Security and Medicare Taxes. Churches making the election do not withhold Social Security or Medicare taxes from employees' wages and do not pay the matching amount. Employees of an electing church pay self-employment tax for any wages over $100 by filing Schedule SE with their Form 1040.

Form 8274 is due prior to the due date of the church's initial Form 941 for the first quarter the church pays wages. Therefore, the election is only available to new churches. The election may be revoked at any time by the church withholding, matching, and remitting the Social Security and Medicare taxes to the IRS.

- **Wages less than $100.** When total wages paid to an employee during a calendar year are less than

ELAINE'S EXTRA
The FICA/Medicare exemption for wages less than $100 is useful when a church determines inadvertent compensation has been paid to a volunteer through appreciation gifts, such as a gift card.

---

[2] IRC Section 3121(w)

$100, there is a special exemption from mandatory withholding and matching of Social Security and Medicare taxes.[3] Wages of less than $100 are generally below the federal tax withholding requirement. With no tax withholdings required, the church is also not required to file Form W-2 for the employee. (See page 95, Reporting Requirements—Form W-2.)

State Obligations

Besides federal registration obligations, churches may have state tax obligations, which include:

- **State Withholding.** Forty-one states have a broad-based income tax which includes the taxation of persons working in a state, both residents of the state and nonresidents. Most states require employers to withhold state income tax as a part of the payroll process and require employers to register with the appropriate state authority. (Note: While federal tax law may exempt ministers from mandatory federal income tax withholding, some states may not have the same exemption available for ministerial employees.)

- **State Unemployment Tax.** While all churches are exempt from the federal unemployment tax (FUTA) based on their statuses as IRC Section 501(c)(3) organizations, states also have their own unemployment tax system. Most states exempt churches from their unemployment tax system.

  While an exemption from state unemployment tax releases churches from a tax burden, it also results in a lack of potential benefits to terminated church workers. The exemption from the state unemployment system should be verified when a church initiates payroll set up. Upon verification, churches should then make efforts to communicate this reality to current and future employees.

- **Workers' Compensation.** Workers' compensation is state-governed. A church should determine if it is required to have workers' compensation insurance and how it is administered. Some states require workers' compensation insurance, and some do not.

  In states like Texas, where workers' compensation is not mandated, churches should consider the consequences of not having this insurance coverage. Churches may want to obtain insurance coverage as a part of risk management plans.

- **New Hire Reporting.** While mandated by federal law and regulated by the US Department of Health & Human Services (HHS), new hire reporting is completed through state reporting. Churches with multistate operations must register with HHS Multistate Employer

---

[3] IRC Section 3121(a)(16)

Registry (MSER) to indicate which state will receive all new hire reporting for the church.[4]

This book does not address all state registration requirements. Churches should seek assistance with obtaining all specific information related to their states' registration requirements.

Trust Fund Taxes and Responsible Persons

In areas of federal and state tax withholding, the church is a fiduciary of their employees' tax funds. This fiduciary responsibility requires great care in complying with all payroll withholding and related deposit rules. Taxes withheld from an employee represent the employees' money. The funds do not belong to the employer. The employer is an intermediary charged with getting the funds to the ultimate party, the IRS. The employees' portion of the payroll taxes is the "trust fund" portion of the payroll tax liability.

The people responsible for making tax deposits, either directly or indirectly, are called "responsible persons." "Responsible persons" possess the authority to decide how the church spends its money, including the payment of tax deposits. A responsible person can be an officer, director, employee, or volunteer. In a church, a responsible person may be the pastor, the treasurer, a member of the finance committee, or a business administrator. There can be multiple responsible persons in any one church.

> **ELAINE'S EXTRA**
>
> Most people view failure to deposit taxes as taking money belonging to the IRS. In reality, failure to deposit taxes is taking money belonging to the employees. The penalties associated with willful failure to deposit are extensive, since in many ways, it is a recovery of stolen funds.

A responsible person may be charged a penalty if the taxes are not deposited timely and the failure is willful.[5] The penalty may be equal to the "trust fund" portion of the taxes. This is one of the few instances where the IRS may assess penalties to the persons working for a corporation as opposed to the penalty being assessed to the corporation. Any "responsible person" penalty is assessed in addition to corporate penalties and interest for late tax deposits.

There is a limited exception from the "responsible persons" definition for voluntary board members of tax exempt organizations,[6] if the board member:

---

[4] For more information go to Office of Child Support Enforcement at https://www.acf.hhs.gov/css/resource/new-hire-reporting-for-employers

[5] IRC Section 6672(a)

[6] IRC Section 6672(e)

1. is solely serving in an honorary capacity;

2. does not participate in the day to day or financial operations of the church; and

3. does not have actual knowledge of the failure on which any penalty is imposed.

The exception cannot be applied if it would leave no "responsible persons" liable for the penalty. The exception provides limited protection for some church volunteers serving as members of a church's governing body, but it does not extend to officers of the church whose defined duties automatically involve them in the day to day operations or the financial operations of the church such as a church's treasurer.

Example 7-1
Bob is First Church's business administrator and Lois is the church's accounting clerk. Lois oversees all payroll processes for the church. Each time payroll is paid, the payroll taxes are recorded as one of the church's bills and the required due date is indicated. Each week, Bob reviews the church's bills and determines which bills are paid, including the timing of the payroll tax deposits. Since Bob has authority to determine the timing of the church's bills, including when the tax deposits are made, he is a "responsible person."

Example 7-2
First Church is experiencing financial difficulties. Lois continues to record the payroll tax liabilities as bills of the church. One week, the church cannot pay all of its bills. Bob instructs Lois to pay the utilities due and the next payroll to the employees, but he waits and later pays the payroll taxes. Bob remains a responsible person. Even though Lois pays the bills (and does not pay the payroll taxes), she is not a responsible person. Lois has no authority to decide when the taxes are deposited.

ELAINE'S EXTRA

Any time an employee is instructed to not make timely tax deposits, they should (1) document the instructions received in writing and (2) prayerfully consider notifying an outside CPA or a person in authority over the decision-maker. This is especially true if the unpaid taxes span several payroll cycles.

Decision-makers must establish systems guaranteeing—no matter the circumstances—the timely deposit of all payroll taxes. Systems should include the procedures needed to make those deposits happen. The decision to pay other bills while payroll taxes go unpaid constitutes a willful failure to pay the payroll taxes.[7]

---

[7]   Howard, 92 AFTR-2d 2003-6389 (301 BR 456)(Bktcy Ct NC) 09/17/2003

Developing procedures to verify tax deposits are made is also important. The decision to trust an employee to make future payroll tax deposits when they have failed to make past payroll tax deposits may also be a willful failure to pay the payroll taxes by the decision-maker and transform the decision-maker into a responsible person.[8] Decision-makers must make sure unpaid taxes are given priority for payment, and they shouldn't trust the job to an employee that has been a part of past tax deposit failures.

Example 7-3

Lou, First Church's treasurer, finds out that Bob has not made the payroll tax deposits and immediately authorizes Lois to make the tax deposits. As the church's treasurer, Lou is already considered a decision-maker of the church. However, Lou is a CPA, and he realizes that his position as a church officer may also make him a potential responsible person for unpaid payroll taxes. Since Bob has shown a lack of judgement by foregoing the tax deposits, Lou instructs Lois to make the payroll tax deposits the same day as payroll is paid and to email him proof of the tax payment. If Lou leaves future tax deposits under Bob's authority and Bob has another lapse in judgement, then Lou's actions may constitute a willful failure to pay the taxes, resulting in a potential penalty to Lou.

Early Decisions to Be Made in Establishing Payroll Systems

Establishing a payroll system requires defining a church's needs and objectives in compensating its workers. When creating a system, churches should analyze the following areas.

Worker Classification

Worker classification, both from an IRS perspective and from a DOL perspective, affects the needs and the objectives of the payroll systems churches use. Payroll systems for employees differ from vendor pay systems for independent contractors—employees require more structure within their respective system than do contractors for theirs. And worker classification in the areas of exempt and nonexempt employees affect the structure of the payroll system to meet wage and hour rules. A church must classify every worker for both IRS and DOL rules (see Chapters 4 and 5).

Pay Periods

Another area of a payroll system that churches should evaluate is pay periods:

---

[8] Erwin v. U.S., 105 AFTR 2d 2010-505 (591 F.3d 313)

- **Regular Pay Periods.** A payroll period is a period of service for which the church pays wages. The options are daily, weekly, bi-weekly, semi-monthly, and monthly. Most state payroll laws don't allow schedules longer than a monthly schedule. The pay period defines the tax withholding tables to be used.

- **Supplemental Wage Payments.** Supplemental wage payments are additional payments, such as bonuses, commissions, awards, prizes, taxable gifts, and taxable fringe benefits. The payments may occur within the regular payroll period or outside of it.

  If supplemental wage payments are paid, a church has three options for calculating federal tax withholdings: (1) pay supplemental wages concurrently with regular wage payments and apply the regular withholding tables; (2) pay supplemental wages separate from regular wage payments and withhold a flat rate of 22[9] percent; or (3) pay supplemental wages separate from regular wage payment and determine additional tax by calculating the tax on previous regular wages plus supplemental wages, then subtract the tax on the previous regular wages. The additional tax is the tax associated with the supplemental wages.[10] Churches should be familiar with these options and decide which option it will use as a general rule for supplemental payments.

> **ELAINE'S EXTRA**
> Daily or weekly payroll schedules can be onerous. Bi-weekly schedules work well and make calculation of overtime easy for nonexempt employees. A semi-monthly schedule is popular when most employees are ministerial or exempt employees.

Example 7-4

Joe is paid a Christmas bonus of $500. Joe's regular pay is $1,000 on the 1st and the 15th of the month. Joe's normal federal income tax withheld is $93.58. The church may calculate the additional tax on the bonus amount using one of these methods:

1. The $500 is added to Joe's regular paycheck on the 15th and the federal tax withholding is calculated according to the tax withholding tables for payroll twice a month on $1,500 for withholding of $153.58;

2. The $500 is paid separate from Joe's regular paycheck on the 15th and the church withholds 22 percent ($110) for federal income tax withholding; or

3. The $500 is paid separate, so the church calculates the tax as it would in Option 1 and compares this to the $93.58 of Joe's normal withholding. The difference

---

9   IRS Notice 1036 (Rev. January 2018)
10   IRS Publication 15

between the two ($60) is attributable to the bonus and is withheld from the bonus payment to Joe.

Payroll Processing System

Determining which payroll system works best for a church is not a one-time decision. A church should revisit this decision if it grows in number of employees or if new payroll operating programs and systems become available. But changing payroll systems is costly, both in time and implementation costs, so care should be taken in selecting a payroll processing system.

Categories of payroll processing systems are:

- **Internal Systems.** Churches use off-the-shelf software applications or simple hand calculations to calculate and perform all payroll functions. Church staff members compute all payroll payments, make tax deposits, and file payroll returns.

  › Pros:

     - Makes advanced funding by the church unnecessary.

     - Retains total control for the church over when the payroll is issued and funded.

     - Retains control over when quarterly and annual payroll reports are filed for the church, providing time to properly review and add in any noncash benefit values.

     - Gives the church the ability to easily deal with payments made outside the regular payroll processing.

  › Cons:

     - Makes the church rely entirely upon staff knowledge of withholding rules and benefit taxation rules.

     - Makes the church rely upon staff to timely submit tax deposits and payroll filings.

     - Requires the church to determine where and when to submit state withholding obligations and state filings.

     - Makes the church responsible for all human resource administration.

- Makes the church adopt and administrate all fringe benefit plans.

- Burdens the church to create backup plans for any unexpected staff absences.

- **External Systems.** Several resources exist for outside payroll processing systems. With an outside processing system, a church still predominantly performs the payroll and human resource duties. The church provides information to the payroll processing service on employees, time worked, fringe benefits, and so on, but the service processes the payroll payments, makes tax deposits, and files all payroll returns.

  › Pros:

    - Ensures the prompt deposits of payroll taxes.

    - Ensures timely, automatic filing of payroll reports.

    - Provides login capabilities for employees to access personal wage and other information.

    - More easily determines state withholding rates.

    - More easily resolves state issues and filings.

    - Offers online availability, which is easy to learn and makes processing from multiple locations possible.

    - Certain systems may create simplicity for churches that do not have accounting staff members—the church just submits time reports and the processor does the rest of the work.

  › Cons:

    - Risks tax-related problems because most outside services do not understand ministerial tax issues or the nuances of tax benefits offered to churches (such as exemption from federal and/or state unemployment taxes).

    - Requires funding two to four days prior to payroll dates.

    - May still place responsibilities on church staff to input data and set up any withholdings or additional pay areas.

    - Places liability on the church if the processing system fails to make tax deposits or file a report, meaning the church is still liable for the amount due or the penalties for failure to comply in a timely manner.

    - Makes corrections difficult because most processors cannot effectively correct errors and may not even take responsibility for errors.

- Limits the amount of time reports and filings are maintained, forcing the church to archive all reports and filings to fulfill its record retention policy.

- Risks a lack of understanding of the special rules applicable to churches for unemployment taxes and various withholding rules.

- Places responsibility on the church for all human resource administration.

- Requires the church to adopt and administrate all fringe benefit plans.

- Produces quick processing of most payroll reports and returns at the end of the quarter or the year, leaving no time to include any taxable fringe benefits generated outside of the payroll system.

- **Professional Employer Organizations (PEOs).** These entities, also called Employee Leasing Arrangements, assume many of the employment and human resource responsibilities of the employer, including the provision and operation of several fringe benefit plans, such as health and retirement plans. A PEO will enter a co-employment arrangement with a church to share the employer responsibilities. The PEO then will be the administrative employer and the church will serve as the worksite employer. The PEO enters into this arrangement with many employers and, as such, has thousands of employees.

  › Pros:

    - Responsibilities for paying wages, payroll- and tax-related filing obligations, and the handling of workers' compensation insurance and related claims falls to the PEO.

    - Relieves the church from registering in multiple states since it is not the "employer" of any workers in other states (the PEO is the employer).

    - Eliminates the need for extensive church staff time setting up and administering fringe benefit plans, such as health insurance, Sec. 125 plans, 401(k) plans, and other benefit plans.

    - Removes the burden from the church to make payroll tax filings on behalf of employees.

    - Upgrades the quality of health insurance plans offered to employees.

    - Often saves the church money because of the cost efficiencies created when the PEO handles payroll, health insurance, and other costs together.

- Provides valuable help with making worker classification determinations.

- Enables employees to access their personal wage and other information when they need it.

- Takes on many of the responsibilities of the human resources department for the church.

- Assists the church with risk management issues that may arise due to employment-related issues, including employee conduct.

- The church has no responsibility for the return filings or payroll tax deposits.

› Cons:

- Requires the church to provide advance funding.

- Eliminates the church's control over payroll functions.

- Makes all wages subject to federal and state unemployment taxes.

- Offers only 401(k) retirement plans—403(b) retirement plans are normally operated outside this type of system.

- Lacks understanding regarding minister tax issues and complications may arise in the areas of housing allowance and FICA/Medicare taxes.

- Likely creates additional work whenever taxable fringe benefits arising out the church's operations must be reported (thus forcing a separate payroll filing by the church and not through the PEO's payroll reporting).

- Ongoing costs for the church—some PEOs charge a flat fee, while some are a percentage of total payroll.

- Duties to track hours worked and provide this information to the PEO fall to the church each pay period.

- Additional costs for processing additional items like bonus payments to employees are likely since they are outside normal pay arrangements.

Common Paymaster Systems

Churches with related organizations sharing employees, such as an affiliated but separately incorporated school, may pursue a common paymaster arrangement. A common paymaster is the corporate member of a group of related corporations responsible for the pay of employees performing specific services for two or more of the related corporations. While the common paymaster remits taxes, each of the employing corporations remains jointly and severally liable for the FICA/Medicare taxes allocable to each organization. Having a common paymaster arrangement allows employees to work for each of the corporate entities with only one FICA wage base application, as opposed to multiple compensation arrangements with each of the corporate entities duplicating the FICA wage base. (Medicare tax has an unlimited wage base, so it is not affected by the arrangement.)

> **Example 7-5**
>
> First Church is affiliated with a separately incorporated school as well as a separately incorporated low-income housing ministry. Bob serves as the business administrator for all three organizations. Bob is not a credentialed minister. The church pays Bob $60,000 per year, the school pays him $50,000 per year and the housing ministry pays him $30,000 per year. If the three organizations operate their own payroll, FICA/Medicare taxes must be paid on all the wages, a total of $140,000, paid to Bob. However, if a common paymaster arrangement is created with First Church as the paymaster, then Bob's total wages will be subject to the FICA wage base of $128,400. The arrangement reduces Bob's withholding of FICA by $719.20 and the employers' tax liability by $719.20. (Total Medicare taxes are the same under both arrangements.)

Timekeeping Systems

How will the church track an employee's work time? As discussed in Chapter 5, a church with nonexempt employees must implement a timekeeping system. The system can be maintained on paper or electronically, using a time clock or other device. Various cloud-based systems allow employees to log on and clock time no matter the work location. Any nonexempt employee must be able to record the time work started and stopped daily, even if the pay arrangement is a salary arrangement with pay consistent from pay period to pay period.

Documents

What documents are needed for the basic payroll system? Churches need to create a basic document package containing the core forms necessary for employment with the church. This package may vary from church to church, but two documents are required for each employee, even if an employee only works for one single day.

- **Form W-4**, Employee's Withholding Allowance Certificate. This form is required for all non-minister employees. It provides a church with the authorization and the information necessary to properly set up an employee's federal tax withholding. Since ministers are exempt from mandatory federal income tax withholding, they do not need to complete the form. If a minister wants federal income tax withheld from his or her pay, he or she may

ELAINE'S EXTRA

Payments to foreign persons present several obstacles. Wage payments to persons ineligible to work in the US may create penalties and mandatory tax payments. Payments may also threaten a person's visa privileges. Any payments to foreign individuals, whether employee or contractor, should be planned for in advance of payment to account for all potential federal requirements related to the payments.

complete the form to indicate the number of withholding allowances. This will serve as an authorization for the church to withhold taxes. A minister may also request a flat amount of withholding through any other written notification to the church.

- **Form I-9**, Employment Eligibility Verification. Only citizens eligible to work in the United States may be employed by a church. Form I-9 is used to verify this eligibility and must be completed by the first date of employment. Failure to obtain a completed Form I-9 and/or hiring ineligible persons may cause penalties.[11] Monetary penalties for failing to produce a Form I-9 range from $110 to $1,100 per violation. Monetary penalties for knowingly hiring and continuing to employ a person ineligible to work in the United States range from $375 to $16,000 per occurrence. Form I-9 is not required for independent contractors.[12]

Tax Deposit Requirements

Deposit Schedules

Taxes withheld from employees must be remitted to the IRS. The IRS maintains two primary tax deposit schedules with one ancillary schedule. The correct deposit schedule is based on a lookback period for the employer and the total tax liability incurred in the lookback period. If a church files Form 941, the lookback period is determined from the total taxes reported on Forms 941, line 10, in a four-quarter lookback period.

Lookback Period

The lookback period begins July 1 and ends June 30 of the year prior to the upcoming calendar year.

---

[11] https://www.ice.gov/factsheets/i9-inspection

[12] Common questions and related answers on the Form I-9 can be viewed at https://www.uscis.gov/i-9-central/questions-and-answers.

Table 1. Example of the lookback period for the calendar year 2019—the four quarters representing July 1, 2017, through June 30, 2018:

3rd Quarter 2017	4th Quarter 2017	1st Quarter 2018	2nd Quarter 2018
July 1, 2017 through September 30, 2017	October 1, 2017 through December 31, 2017	January 1, 2018 through March 31, 2018	April 1, 2018 through June 30, 2018

Deposit Schedule

- **Monthly.** A church is a monthly depositor if the total taxes for its lookback period are $50,000 or less. Tax deposits are due by the 15th day of the calendar month following the calendar month the taxes are withheld.

- **Semiweekly.** A church is a semiweekly depositor if the total taxes for its lookback period are greater than $50,000. For a semiweekly depositor, the schedule is:

Table 2. Semiweekly Deposit Schedule

If the payday falls on a …	… then deposit taxes by the following:
Wednesday, Thursday, and/or Friday	Wednesday
Saturday, Sunday, Monday, and/or Tuesday	Friday

- **Daily.** If, at any time, the total taxes withheld and not deposited exceed $100,000, the taxes must be deposited the next business day.

All deposits are due only on business days. If a deposit day is not a business day (i.e., a holiday), the deposit is due on the following business day. Saturdays, Sundays, and legal holidays are not business days.

Warning: *When using the IRS EFTPS system, understand the payment cut-off times built into the system. Payments may have to be scheduled for a future date. Care should be taken to know cut-off dates and posting times to avoid a late payment.*

Late Deposit Penalties

Late deposits are subject to penalties. These penalties can be substantial and are rarely abated by the IRS. Reflecting the seriousness of failure to remit payroll penalties, penalties

ELAINE'S EXTRA

Failure to deposit payroll
taxes is a common weakness
in churches. It is easy to put
off making the tax deposit
in favor of paying other
expenses. While the above
deposit schedules are the legal
requirements, inadvertent
errors are avoided if payroll
taxes are always deposited the
same day that payroll is issued.

will be assessed even when failure to deposit is due
to employee theft or malfeasance.

For amounts not properly or timely deposited, the
penalty rates are:

- **2 percent** for deposits made 1 to 5 days late

- **5 percent** for deposits made 6 to 15 days late

- **10 percent** for deposits made 16 or more days late,
  but before 10 days from the date of the first notices
  the IRS sent asking for the tax due

- **10 percent** for amounts that should have been
  deposited, but instead were paid directly to the
  IRS, or paid with the payroll tax return

- **15 percent** for amounts still unpaid more than 10
days after the date of the first notice the IRS sent asking for the tax due or the day on
which a church received notice and demand for immediate payment, whichever is earlier.

Reporting Requirements

Every church must be familiar with the payroll tax return reporting requirements, which include:

Form 944 – Employer's Annual Federal Tax Return

For small churches anticipating tax withholdings of
$2,500 or less, Form 944 may be filed annually. The
IRS will notify a church if it qualifies to file Form 944. If
a church has not received this notification, it must file
Form 941. If a church wants to file Form 944, it may
request to be classified as a Form 944 employer. Form
944 is due January 31 for the preceding calendar year.

Form 941 - Employer's Quarterly Federal Tax Return

Most churches file Form 941 to report wages and related
tax obligations. Form 941 is filed on a quarterly basis.
The return is due by the last day of the month following
the end of a calendar quarter. Form 941 may be elec-

ELAINE'S EXTRA

To provide assurance that
management is aware of
any failure in this area of
administration, a church
may complete Form 2848
naming an officer, a CPA,
or an attorney as the power
of attorney (POA). The
POA will receive copies
of correspondence from
the IRS regarding payroll
tax returns, payments, or
amounts unpaid.

tronically filed or filed on paper.[13]

Table 3. Form 941 Due Dates

Quarter 1: **January 1 – March 31**	Due Date: **April 30**
Quarter 2: **April 1 – June 30**	Due Date: **July 31**
Quarter 3: **July 1 – September 30**	Due Date: **October 31**
Quarter 4: **October 1 – December 31**	Due Date: **January 31**

Penalties for Late Filing of Form 941 or Form 944

Failure to file will result in 5 percent of the unpaid tax, due with the return for any month, or part of a month that the return is not filed, up to a maximum of 25 percent.

Failure to pay will result in 0.5 percent of the unpaid tax for any month or part of a month that the tax remains unpaid.

Form W-2 – Wage and Tax Statement

Form W-2 should be issued to employees. This form reports wages paid, taxes collected, and sometimes fringe benefits. Form W-2 is required when:

- Any amount is withheld for income, Social Security, or Medicare tax from the wages, regardless of the amount of wages paid;

- Withholding for income tax would have been required had the employee claimed no more than one withholding allowance or had not claimed exemption from withholding on Form W-4; or

- $600 or more was paid in wages, even if no tax was required to be withheld.

ELAINE'S EXTRA

Prior to filing the fourth quarter Form 941 and the annual Forms W-2, a church must review all benefits provided to staff members to identify any taxable benefits that need to be reported. Further discussions on fringe benefit programs are contained in Chapters 8 and 9.

ELAINE'S EXTRA

For small churches, the electronic filing system hosted by the Social Security Administration provides an easy and inexpensive method of electronically filing Forms W-2.

---

[13] For more information see
www.irs.gov/employmentefile.

Due Date. Forms W-2 are due to the Social Security Administration by January 31 for the prior calendar year (i.e., 2018 Forms W-2 are due January 31, 2019). This is the due date for both paper filings and electronic filings. An extension of time to file may be obtained by filing Form 8809 to request a 30-day extension. If a church is filing 250 or more Forms W-2, the Forms W-2 must be filed electronically.

Penalties for Failure to File Forms W-2 or Furnish Correct Statements to Payees

Penalties may be assessed either for failing to file Forms W-2 with the government or for failing to provide the forms to employees. To avoid penalties, churches should take care to file the returns timely with both the Social Security Administration and their employees. Penalties are

- Filed within 30 days of the due date - $50 per return

- Filed 31 days late but by August 1 - $100 per return

- Filed after August 1 or not at all - $260 per return

- Intentional disregard for filing requirements - $530 per return

Form W-3 – Transmittal of Wage and Tax Statements

Form W-3 is a summary of all wage statements (i.e., Forms W-2). Paper Forms W-2 should be submitted to the Social Security Administration with Form W-3.

Form W-3/Form 941/944 Reconciliation

The Social Security Administration and the Internal Revenue Service share information regarding wage payments. Each year the IRS compares the amounts reported for Social Security wages and Medicare wages on Forms 941 Lines 5a and 5c/Form 944 Lines 4a and 4c to the amounts reported on Form W-3 in boxes 3 and 5. If these amounts are different, the IRS or the Social Security Administration will send an inquiry to the church to request an explanation of the differences. Every church should perform this reconciliation prior to filing the Forms W-2 and the fourth quarter Form 941 for the year to detect any potential problems prior to completing the annual filings.

CHAPTER 7 KEY POINTS:

- Payroll is a complicated process and churches must invest the time and resources to create a system complying with all regulations and requirements.

- Decision makers may be personally liable for penalties when payroll taxes are not deposited with the IRS.

- Various options for performing the payroll function are available, and each church should determine the best fit for its staff experience, availability, and finances.

- Awareness of all deposit and filing deadlines is crucial to administering the payroll process and keep the church free from penalties.

BENEFITS – MORE THAN JUST THE PAYCHECK

Understanding fringe benefits and identifying core concepts allowing for tax advantages

In the past few years, the Internal Revenue Service has conducted compliance initiatives involving nonprofit organizations. In two of the initiatives, the IRS determined significant deficiencies by employers in the reporting of fringe benefits and perks provided to employees (primarily key employees involved with the organization's leadership and management duties). In a compliance project involving colleges and universities, for instance, the IRS initiated 11 employment tax exams. These exams resulted in increases of $35.5 million in taxable wages, $7.1 million in employment taxes, and $167,242.90 in penalties.[1]

While these compliance initiatives did not include churches, they generally reveal how common these errors are among employers, including nonprofit employers. My experiences working with churches throughout the past 30 years confirms that virtually every church suffers from reporting deficiencies with fringe benefit reporting.

Treating fringe benefits correctly begins with gaining a basic understanding of the tax concepts underlying fringe benefits. Learning to recognize common errors associated with providing fringe benefits may assist a church in avoiding the potential hazards created by these errors.

General Rule of Taxation

Understanding the taxation of fringe benefits begins with understanding the core concept of the US tax code. Everything benefiting or providing value to an individual (employee) is tax-

---

[1] IRS Exempt Organizations Colleges and Universities Compliance Project https://www.irs.gov/pub/irs-tege/CUCP_FinalRpt_050213.pdf

able to the individual unless the Internal Revenue Code specifically excludes the benefit from taxation.[2] Unfortunately, most tax-exempt organizations, including churches, do not understand this concept. Income is more than the cash components of a compensation package. Not recognizing the additional potential areas of taxable income leads to a risk of unreported wages, unpaid federal and state income taxes, unpaid employment taxes, interest, penalties, intermediate sanctions and, in extreme circumstances, jail time for an employee.[3]

Common Sources of Errors in Recognizing Taxable Benefits

Use of Church Assets

Churches often believe they are making up for low wages by giving employees fringe benefits. Handled incorrectly, these intended blessings can turn into burdens for both the church and the employee. Some churches altruistically allow their employees the use of certain church assets without charging the employees. A perk like this one usually creates taxable income for the employee.

Example 8-1
Betty is the youth minister at First Church. To make Betty's job easier, First Church allows her two-year-old son to attend the church's daycare without charge. The church believes it is helping Betty and her young family's limited income. However, Betty is the only staff member allowed this privilege. Therefore, the value of her son's daycare must be included on Betty's Form W-2 as taxable income.

ELAINE'S EXTRA
The value of Betty's daycare is not taxable—if First Church institutes an IRC Section 129 dependent care plan. These plans are discussed in Chapter 9.

Protection of a Church's Assets

Churches may take actions to protect certain assets by making arrangements with employees, not realizing a taxable benefit is created in the process.

Example 8-2
First Church doesn't want to leave its van in the church parking lot overnight. The church allows Ed, the maintenance man, to drive the van to and from work so that it is not left on the premises overnight. During the day, the van is used by various employees and volunteers for church purposes. Although the church is protecting its asset, it fails

---

[2] IRC Section 61(a)

[3] U.S. v. Clarke, 103 AFTR 2d 2009-1349 (562 F.3d 1158), (CA11) 3/20/2009 – served 21 months in jail for tax evasion when his tax return simply reported what was on his Form W-2 and Forms 1099-Misc which omitted $110,000 of taxable fringe benefits.

to realize that the commuting value of the van is taxable to Ed and must be included on his Form W-2.[4]

Required Participation

Churches may desire for ministers or employees to participate in certain church activities. In order to make such an expectation affordable for the employee, a church pays for certain activities directly or provides a discount. It is a common misconception that if the church asks an employee to participate or use a service of the church, then it automatically does not need to be counted as compensation. It can whenever the benefit is provided to some employees, but not all. However, just requiring an employee to participate in an activity does not create a tax-free benefit.

> **ELAINE'S EXTRA**
> Tax-free tuition reductions may be provided to certain staff members under a qualified tuition reduction plan defined by IRC Section 117. See Chapter 9 for a discussion of these plans.

Example 8-3

First Church requires its senior pastor to enroll his children in the church's elementary school. The church believes it is important for the pastor to show he supports the school, but it also recognizes the added expense this imposes on the pastor, so it grants him a 100-percent tuition discount. The tuition discount is not offered to other employees. Since First Church does not have a qualifying tuition reduction plan, the amount of the discount becomes taxable income for the pastor.

Example 8-4

A church believes it is important for its ministers' children to attend church camp each year. So that the requirement does not create a financial burden, the church pays the camp fees for the ministers' children. There is no fringe benefit plan allowing for this type of arrangement, so the value of the camp must be added to the ministers' Forms W-2.

Imitating Other Churches

One of the biggest mistakes churches make is to imitate how other churches handle fringe benefits for tax purposes without gaining all of the facts first.

Example 8-5

Pastor Joe of First Church learns that Pastor Tom at Second Church receives an auto

---

4 Reg. §1.61-21(f)

allowance. Pastor Joe believes this is a great idea and requests one. Since the benefit is an "allowance" and is for "business" expenses, he does not believe it should be included in his taxable income. He assumes Pastor Tom isn't paying tax on his auto allowance, but is unaware that Pastor Tom's allowance is properly added to his Form W-2 each year as a taxable benefit.

In Summary

Churches cannot create their own basis for tax-exempt perks and fringe benefits. Every benefit must be analyzed under the tax code to determine its tax status and to avoid underreporting of employees' income.

Cash or Benefit? Providing a Choice Makes a Difference

A fringe benefit is defined as an "incidental or additional advantage, (especially) a benefit provided by an employer to supplement an employee's regular pay, such as a pension, company car, luncheon vouchers, etc."[5] Fringe benefits are extras—things added to cash compensation, and not instead of cash compensation.

A fringe benefit's taxation can be affected by how it is provided to one or more employees. Favorable tax treatment of a benefit generally occurs when the benefit is made in addition to a cash compensation plan and not instead of cash compensation. Where an employee may take a benefit, or take the cash equivalent of the benefit, the taxation of the fringe benefit for that employee (and sometimes for all employees) may be altered. This type of arrangement is known as a "cash or benefit" plan.

Churches can create "cash or benefit" plans through two options.

OPTION ONE: Allowing employees a choice of taking extra cash in their paycheck or taking the benefit

When an employee can choose between taking a benefit and taking the cash value of the benefit, the benefit is usually taxable to the employee. This arrangement with one employee may make all benefits taxable to all employees, even those who are not provided the choice. For example, all health insurance premiums can become taxable to all employees as illustrated in following example.

---

[5] Fringe benefit. (n.d.). *Collins English Dictionary - Complete & Unabridged 10th Edition.* Retrieved January 8, 2018 from Dictionary.com website http://www.dictionary.com/browse/fringe-benefit

Example 8-6

First Church hires Bob as its business administrator. First Church provides health insurance to its employees through a group health insurance plan. The premiums paid by the church for the group health insurance plan are not taxable to First Church's employees. Bob doesn't need health insurance because he and his family are covered by his wife's health insurance plan through her employer. Because Bob doesn't need the health insurance, First Church agrees to pay him the equivalent of the health insurance premiums as additional salary. The arrangement creates a "cash or benefit" plan.

In Example 8-6, Bob is offered health insurance or the cash value of the health insurance. Because of the ability to choose, Bob faces taxable income whether he chooses the insurance or the cash. An additional concern is created because the choice given to Bob may affect the taxability of the health insurance premiums provided to other employees even though they are not provided with the same choice as Bob.

OPTION TWO: Offering benefits paid through salary deductions

Cash or benefit plans are not only created by choices provided with employer funds. Cash or benefit plans may be created when choices are provided to employees on benefits paid using employee funds.

Example 8-7

First Church hires Bob as its business administrator. First Church provides health insurance to its employees through a group health insurance plan and pays for the employees' premiums. Bob accepts the insurance plan for him and his family. The church pays for Bob's premiums, but he must pay for the family coverage portion of the premium. Bob enrolls in the health insurance and elects to pay for his family's coverage through payroll deduction. As in Example 8-6, the arrangement creates another type of "cash or benefit" plan. (Bob would have the cash if not for his election to pay for the benefit.)

Providing employees with the option of utilizing payroll deductions to fund the cost of benefit plans provides employees with a choice on the use of the funds creating a "cash or benefit" plan. In these arrangements, the follow-up step is to determine if amounts withheld through a payroll deduction plan are treated as pre-tax or post-tax amounts.

Pre-Tax or Post-Tax

For an employee paying for a fringe benefit, a church must determine when and if tax will be calculated on the dollars used to pay for the fringe benefit. Churches must understand some important terms used in this area.

Elective Deferral/Salary Reduction. An elective deferral or salary reduction exists when an employer withholds or deducts funds from an employee's paycheck to pay for benefits or to place in a benefit plan.

Post-Tax. A deferral or reduction is a "post-tax" deduction when taxes are calculated before the deduction is taken out of the pay.

Example 8-8

In Example 8-7, Bob elected to have the amount for his family's health insurance of $250 deducted from his paycheck. His gross pay per pay period is $1,500. The deduction is a post-tax deduction, so Bob's taxes are calculated on $1,500.

Pre-Tax. A deferral or reduction is a "pre-tax" deduction when taxes are calculated after the deduction is taken from the pay.

Example 8-9

In Example 8-7, Bob elected to have the amount for his family's health insurance of $250 deducted from his paycheck. Since First Church operates a Section 125 cafeteria plan, employees' deductions are pre-tax. Bob's gross pay per period is $1,500. Because of the Section 125 plan, the deduction is a pre-tax deduction, so Bob's taxes are calculated on $1,250.

As illustrated in Example 8-9, it is possible to create "cash or benefit" plans allowing for the tax-favorable treatment of benefits. In Example 8-9, the church operates a Section 125 cafeteria plan. The plan creates the "pre-tax" treatment of the deduction. Avoiding adverse tax consequences requires a qualifying fringe benefit plan with strict operating requirements. Some benefits provide for a "pre-tax" plan to be created and other benefits may not be offered on a "pre-tax" basis without using "cash or benefit" plans commonly known as Cafeteria Plans or Section 125 Plans, which is named after the Internal Revenue Code Section that authorized the plans.

Section 125 – Cafeteria Plans

Cafeteria plans allow churches to offer many benefits pre-tax, either through employee payroll deductions or through an employer's funding of the benefits. Benefits offered through the plan are generally not subject to federal income tax or Social Security/Medicare taxes. Certain categories of benefits may be subject to taxes, even if offered through a cafeteria plan. Group term life insurance in excess of $50,000 and adoption assistance are subject to Social Security/Medicare taxes even if offered through a cafeteria plan.

Warning: *A cafeteria plan does not exist until a church has adopted a written cafeteria plan.*

Until the document is adopted and signed, employees may not claim benefits under the plan.

Example 8-10

Bob, First Church's business administrator, wants his payroll deductions for his portion of the health insurance to be deducted pre-tax. Working with a third-party employee benefits consulting company, Bob drafts the church's plan document. The plan document is presented to the finance committee for consideration. The finance committee adopts the plan and has it signed on January 31, 2019. The benefits of the plan may not be claimed until after January 31, 2019.

Plan Requirements

Strict operating rules apply to cafeteria plans, including:

- The plan is operated for the benefit of employees. Workers classified as independent contractors are not eligible for the plan;

- The plan is a separate written plan document containing specified information, and it must be signed and adopted by the church;

- The benefits offered do not defer compensation to the following year outside specific perimeters, which generally results in a "use it or lose it" feature of the plan. (Plans may institute a two-and-a-half-month grace period for certain benefits);

- The operation of the plan may not discriminate in favor of highly compensated employees[6]—highly compensated is defined as employees making $120,000[7] or more;

- The employees' elections are irrevocable and can only be changed by the occurrence of defined situations both covered by the plan document[8] and legally defined by the Internal Revenue Code.

> **ELAINE'S EXTRA**
>
> While cafeteria plans do not require the use of a trust to segregate the funds, I strongly advise using a third-party administrator to administer the funds. An administrator assists in tracking the deferrals into the plan and processing the claims by the employees. In many instances, the tax savings from the plan will assist in paying administration costs. If the church is covered by ERISA or adopts a plan document that incorporates ERISA, the church must engage a third-party administrator.

---

[6] Highly compensated is defined by IRC Section 414(q)(1).

[7] This amount may be indexed for cost of living adjustments. For plan years beginning in 2018, the amount is $120,000.

[8] Treas. Reg. Section 1.125-4(b)-(g)

The benefits allowed in cafeteria plans can vary, including:

- Medical insurance (including dental and vision);

- Dependent care—not to exceed $5,000 per year;

- Medical expense reimbursement;

- Adoption assistance;

- Health savings account, but not if the participant elects the medical expense reimbursement;

- Group term life insurance less than or equal to $50,000 of coverage (tax-free from all taxes);

- Group term life insurance greater than $50,000 (subject to Social Security/Medicare taxes)[9];

- Long- and short-term disability coverage.

Not all benefits qualify for cafeteria plans, though, including the following exclusions:

- Individual insurance plans;

- Retirement plans;

- Archer Medical Savings Accounts (special trust accounts for employees of small employers or self-employed individuals);

- Athletic facilities;

- Educational assistance;

- Employee discounts;

- Cell phones;

- Meals;

- Lodging on business premises;

- Moving expenses;

> **ELAINE'S EXTRA**
> Many churches establish a simple cafeteria plan only offering medical insurance premium payments to allow the employee to pay for his/her share of employer-provided accident and health insurance premiums. These churches still must determine whether the premium-only cafeteria plan complies with the requirements of the Affordable Care Act and the geneeral rules of IRC Section 125.

---

[9] The "cost" of the group term life insurance greater than $50,000 must be valued according to IRC Section 79 and added to an employee's income, if the insurance is paid using an employee's pre-tax salary reduction contributions to a cafeteria plan.

- Transportation;

- Tuition reduction;

- Working condition benefits (discussed in Chapter 9).

Note: The above benefits may not be included in the structure of a cafeteria plan, but there are still special provisions allowing for the benefits to be provided in a tax advantageous manner.

Cafeteria plans offer an excellent avenue for tax-advantaged payment of fringe benefits. The rules are complicated and far exceed the discussion in this chapter. Experienced professional assistance is necessary when drafting and implementing a cafeteria plan. Additionally, a church must review its plan regularly, including annual reviewing of benefits provided through the plan, to maintain compliance with the plan.

CHAPTER 8 KEY POINTS:

- Understanding general tax concepts of fringe benefits is necessary to identify taxable fringe benefits and to provide benefits through tax-advantageous plans.

- Tax law determines the taxation of a benefit and not the church's good intentions.

- Offering a choice between cash and a benefit always creates a tax consequence—most often an adverse one without proper planning.

- Deductions from employees' paychecks to pay for benefits are not automatically pre-tax deductions.

- Cafeteria plans provide an excellent avenue to allow employees to fund the cost of benefit plans using pre-tax dollars.

WORK-RELATED FRINGE BENEFITS

Structuring benefits related to the job to achieve maximum tax benefits

Churches may use various cash and noncash arrangements to compensate employees beyond regular cash compensation. Generally, arrangements outside of regular compensation arrangements are referred to as fringe benefits. Fringe benefits, granted preferable tax treatment, may fall into one of two categories: (1) work-related fringe benefits (covered in this chapter) and (2) life-related fringe benefits (see Chapter 10).

Work-related fringe benefits involve events or circumstances directly tied to the employer. There are rules governing these benefits—more than just that they must be associated with working conditions. Churches rarely realize this.

Common examples of where churches usually are unaware of benefit rules include:

- Paying for parking near the church;

- Providing a discount at the church bookstore;

- Providing a cell phone to an employee; and

- Paying for educational or training expenses.

As discussed in Chapter 8, churches must look at **all** benefits and determine how they fit within the tax code for exclusion or as taxable income to the employee. In determining the legal authority for excluding benefits from income, Internal Revenue Code Section 132 excludes many common, and often overlooked, benefits. However, there are rules a church must follow to gain and keep the tax exclusions.

Fringe benefits covered by IRC Section 132 fall into the following categories:

- "No-additional-cost services";

- Qualified employee discounts for products and services;

- Working condition fringe, such as job-related mileage or education;

- De minimis fringe benefits, such as occasional use of church's copier for personal purposes;

- Qualified transportation fringes;

- On-site gyms or athletic facilities;

- Qualified moving expense reimbursements (suspended for 2018 through 2025);[1] and

- Qualified retirement planning services.

As churches review benefits provided to employees, keep this in mind: There is an overriding rule that any fringe benefit covered by another specific portion of the Code may not be covered under IRC Section 132.[2] For example, discounts at a church-related school are not a qualified discount under IRC Section 132 since education discounts are governed by IRC Section 117. Therefore, in applying IRC Section 132 to fringe benefits, it is important to confirm that the benefit is not covered by another provision of the Code.

No-Additional-Cost Services

The "no-additional-cost services" provision[3] allows staff members to freely utilize services the church provides to the general public as a part of its regular operations. Employees may utilize the services without creating income, if the church does not incur substantial additional costs in providing the services to the employee.

> ### Example 9-1
> First Church operates a Christian camp. Each summer it opens enrollment to the public and establishes its cost based on projected enrollment. During the summer, it allows the church's staff to enroll their children in one of the camp programs as unexpected availability occurs, either due to cancellations or unsold space at any camp. All staff members may participate in the program by placing their children on the waiting list. First Church offers the program free to its staff. The value of the camp is not taxable to the staff member, since it meets the criteria of a "no-additional-cost" service.

Warning: *If the church allowed all the staff's children to go to camp for free during the open enrollment period without restriction, the program would not qualify as a "no-additional-cost" service.*

---

[1]   IRC Section 132(g)(2)
[2]   IRC Section 132(l)
[3]   IRC Section 132(a) and 132(b)

Churches can run afoul of the benefit's provisions by assuming it applies when it does not apply.

Example 9-2

First Church's youth minister, Betty, has a 3-year-old child. The church operates a day-care and allows Betty to enroll her toddler for free. The church believes it does not have any additional costs associated with adding one more child to the program, since it has space in the daycare. First Church does not add the value of the daycare to Betty's income. However, the value of the daycare is taxable because the "no-additional-cost" services provision may not be applied to the provision of dependent care, a benefit governed by IRC Section 129.

Restrictions

"No-additional-cost" services may not discriminate in favor of highly compensated[4] employees and must be provided on substantially the same terms to all the employees of an appropriate class.[5] In Example 9-2, providing the daycare to only one staff member, Betty, does not meet this test.

Any benefit specifically covered under its own provision of the IRC may not be covered by an IRC Section 132 benefit.[6] As demonstrated in Example 9-2, dependent care benefits are covered under a different Code section, and providing Betty with daycare assistance is not an eligible "no-additional-cost" services benefit.

Allowable Recipients

No-additional-cost services may be provided to "employees." For purposes of this benefit, "employees" are defined to include:[7]

- Any individual currently employed by the church;

- Any individual formerly employed by the church but separated from service due to

> **ELAINE'S EXTRA**
>
> Churches, especially smaller churches, may report ministers' wages on Form 1099-MISC because they believe this is easier and that it doesn't matter what form is used to report the minister's wages. Using Form 1099-MISC forfeits a minister's eligibility for tax-free benefits under the no-additional-cost services, qualified employee discounts, or on-site athletic facilities rules.

---

[4] "Highly compensated" may have different meanings for different tax related subjects. For IRC Section 132, it is defined by IRC Section 414(q).

[5] IRC Section 132(j)(1)

[6] IR Reg. Sec. 1.132-1(f)(1)

[7] IRC Section 132(h)

retirement or disability;

- Any widow or widower of the two groups listed above; and

- Any spouse or dependent child of the persons listed above.

Qualified Employee Discounts

Churches commonly offer discounts to employees on services or products sold by the church. Employees receive a discount at the church's bookstore or are allowed a reduced rate to a program or class. However, few churches realize there are limits on the discounts that can be provided tax-free as a qualified employee discount.[8]

For product sold, the discount may not exceed the gross profit percentage of the price at which the item is being offered by the employer to customers. For services offered, the discount may not exceed 20 percent.[9]

Example 9-3

First Church operates a bookstore. The church's general operating policy is to set prices at 200 percent of the cost of the item to the church. Usually the policy provides a gross profit percentage of 50 percent. Church employees enjoy a 10-percent discount on all purchases. The discount program is less than the gross profit percentage and is a qualified employee discount.

Example 9-4

First Church operates an active and thriving music department. Encouraging people to embrace music, it offers several classes on various musical instruments. Classes are $45 for a 30-minute lesson. A 10-percent discount is offered to church employees. Since the discount is less than 20 percent, it is a qualified employee discount.

Restrictions

The IRS states that qualified employee discounts may not discriminate in favor of highly compensated[10] employees and must be provided on substantially the same terms to all the employees of an appropriate class.[11]

Also, any benefit specifically covered under its own provision of the Code may not be cov-

---

[8]   IRC Sections 132(a) and 132(c)
[9]   IRC Section 132(c)(1)
[10]   "Highly compensated" may have different meanings for different tax related subjects. For IRC
        Section 132, it is defined by IRC Section 414(q).
[11]   IRC Section 132(j)(1)

ered by IRC Section 132 benefits.[12] For example, there are other code sections that provide specific plans for discounts related to childcare and tuition.

Example 9-5

First Church operates an elementary school. The church allows all employees a 15-percent discount on the school's tuition. Even though the discount is less than 20 percent, First Church may not consider the 15-percent discount as a tax-free qualified employee discount. Tuition discounts are covered under IRC Section 117. First Church must review the discount under the rules of IRC Section 117 to determine if the discount is taxable or nontaxable to the employee. It may not consider the discount to be a qualified employee discount under IRC Section 132.

ELAINE'S EXTRA

A special warning about "classes" is appropriate. Selecting a "class" of employees for benefit programs should be carefully considered. If a class is so small that the member(s) of the class can be readily named, the class is probably not an appropriate class. This generally occurs when churches create the class of "ministers." The smaller the church, the less likely that ministers may create an appropriate class for benefit plans.

Allowable Recipients

Qualified employee discounts may be provided to "employees." For purposes of this benefit, "employees" are defined to include:[13]

- Any individual currently employed by the church;

- Any individual formerly employed by the church but has separated from service due to retirement or disability;

- Any widow or widower of the two groups listed above; and

- Any spouse or dependent child of the persons listed above.

Working Condition Fringe

Another type of fringe benefit is a working condition fringe. This is defined as any property or services provided to an employee that would be deductible as a business expense if the

---

[12] IR Reg. Sec. 1.132-1(f)(1)
[13] IRC Section 132(h)

employee directly paid for it.[14] Fringe benefits in this category are commonly expenses covered by a church's accountable expense reimbursement plan. The expenses are closely aligned with an employee's job and are rarely referred to or considered a "fringe" benefit. This category may include many different types of expenses, but some expenses covered by this provision are noteworthy:

- *Business mileage.* This provision never includes commuting or any expense covered by the qualified transportation benefit rules discussed later in this chapter.

   Example 9-6

   Joe is the children's minister at First Church. First Church has two campuses and Joe's duties regularly take him between the two campuses. Joe's mileage between the two campuses is business mileage and may be paid by the church.

- *Continuing education or training.* Continuing education or training enables staff members to do their jobs better but does not qualify them for a new line of work. These education expenses differ from general education expenses provided through an educational assistance plan under IRC Section 127. (For a comparison of educational assistance plans and continuing education plans, see the Appendix on page 169 and a discussion of educational assistance plans in Chapter 10.)

   Example 9-7

   Joe is required by First Church to attend two conferences each year related to his role as the children's minister. The conferences are continuing education required for Joe to maintain his job and may be paid by the church.

   Example 9-8

   Joe is working on his doctorate at the local theological seminary. First Church encourages Joe's doctorate work, believing it makes him a better minister. However, since a doctorate qualifies Joe for a new position (even if he does not want a new position) the expenses for the doctorate education may not be paid by the church unless they are included in Joe's income.[15]

- *Cell phones.* Cell phones may be provided tax-free when provided for bona fide business purposes of the church, and not as an item of compensation.[16] The reason for providing the cell phone should be clearly explained in an employment agreement or a job

---

[14] IRC Section 132(d)
[15] *See* Czarnecki, Jr. v. U.S., 120 AFTR 2d 2017-6173, (Ct Fed Cl,), 10/13/2017 for a discussion on the disallowance of expenses associated with doctoral program costs.
[16] IRS Notice 2011-72, 2011-36 IRB 407

description. If the church reimburses the cost of the cell phone or provides an allowance, an employee should provide documentation supporting the existence of the expense. (A sample policy for this purpose is provided on page 172.)

Example 9-9

First Church operates on a large campus with multiple buildings covering five acres. Sam, the head of maintenance, may be at any place on the campus at any point in time. The church provides Sam with a cell phone to make it convenient to reach him throughout the day. Since there is a business reason for providing the cell phone, the church may provide the cell phone tax-free to Sam.

Example 9-10

First Church is preparing a job offer for Susie as the children's department coordinator. Susie's duties will occur at the church during regular operating hours and she will be provided an office to perform her job. As a part of her job offer, the church includes providing her a cell phone. Since Susie's duties will not require her to have a cell phone, and the cell phone is linked to her compensation in her job offer, the value of the cell phone may <u>not</u> be excluded from Susie's taxable compensation as a working condition fringe benefit.

- *Business purpose travel.* Expenses for travel where the primary purpose is to conduct the church's business are a tax-free working condition fringe benefit.

Example 9-11

Joe is attending one of his required conferences (Example 9-7) at a wonderful resort and brings his wife. Joe's cost to attend the conference, including hotel, meals, and travel, are a working condition fringe benefit. The costs associated with Joe's wife are personal and may not be provided by the church. However, unless the hotel costs are increased by having another person stay in the hotel room, the cost of the room is a working condition fringe benefit.

> ### ELAINE'S EXTRA
> Costs associated with a spouse to travel will always be personal unless the spouse is conducting church business for a substantial portion of the trip. Many churches desire spouses to travel with ministers for accountability and appearance reasons. While these reasons may be logical, they are insufficient to convert a spouse's portion of the travel expenses into business expenses.

Restrictions

For expenses to be considered a working condition fringe benefit, they must meet the criteria for deduction under Code Section 162 as ordinary and necessary expenses incurred for the church's operations and must be properly documented as required by the IRS, including the more extensive documentation requirements of Code Section 274 for travel, meals, gifts, entertainment, and auto expenses.   IRS Publication 463 provides a further discussion of the documentation requirements for Code Section 274 expenses. Chapter 7 of the *Church and Clergy Tax Guide* provides a discussion of business expenses.

Certain expenses may be provided in a manner that provides a working condition fringe benefit as well as a personal benefit with a taxable component. These types of expenses must be evaluated in advance to determine the appropriate tax classification. Common expenses containing a personal element include:

- Employer provided autos

- Flights on employer-owned aircraft

- Security services

- On-site employer provided dining facilities

Allowable Recipients

Working condition fringe benefits are available to these groups of workers:

- A current employee;

- A director; and

- An independent contractor.

De Minimis Fringe

The term "de minimis fringe" means any property or service of so little value that accounting for it would be difficult. These are the little things a church does for its employees. They are low in value and/or they infrequently occur. De minimis fringe benefits are often utilized by churches without thought to rules or boundaries.

Included in this category of benefits are:[17]

- Occasional use of a copier or a fax machine;

- Occasional office or group parties for employees;

---

[17]   Treas.Reg. Section 1.132-6(e)

- Personal use of the church computer and internet access;

- Traditional birthday or Christmas gifts of property with a low fair market value;

- Occasional theater tickets or occasional sporting event tickets;

- Coffee, doughnuts, and soft drinks; and

- Flowers, fruit, books, or other similar property at special times or special circumstances, such as birthdays or funerals.

All the excludable items on the above list are items of property. A cash benefit or cash equivalent (such as a gift card) is <u>never</u> excluded as a fringe benefit.[18] This is true even if the item to be purchased with the cash would be excluded as a de minimis fringe benefit. Other items that may not be excluded from income as a de minimis fringe benefit include:[19]

- Season theater or season sporting event tickets;

- Memberships in private clubs or athletic facilities;

- Use of employer-owned facilities, such as apartments, lodges, and boats; and

- Commuting use of an employer-provided automobile.

> **Example 9-12**
> First Church loves to celebrate its employees. At each employee's birthday, it gives them a fruit basket and two tickets to the local movie theater. The total value of the gift is normally $45 to $50. The gift qualifies as a de minimis fringe benefit.

> **Example 9-13**
> First Church loves to celebrate its employees. At each employee's birthday, it gives a gift card for $50. The gift card does <u>not</u> qualify as a de minimis fringe benefit and must be treated as taxable income.

> **Example 9-14**
> First Church received a donation of a time-share located on the beach in Destin, Florida. Employees can use the time-share for vacations. The time-share is an employer-owned facility and is not a de minimis fringe benefit.

Restrictions and Allowable Recipients

Due to the low-value nature of de minimis fringe benefits, they may be provided to any

---

[18] Treas. Reg. Section 1.132-6(c)
[19] Treas. Reg. Section 1.132(e)(2)

employee and are not limited by nondiscrimination rules. These are also the types of benefits that may be provided to volunteers without creating tax ramifications.

Special Types of De Minimis Fringe Benefits

Meals at an employer-operated eating facility. The value of meals provided to employees at an employer-operated eating facility may be considered a de minimis fringe benefit if:

- The facility is located on the church's business premises;

- The revenue generated from the facility equals or exceeds the direct operating costs of the facility; and

- The facility is not operated in favor of highly compensated employees.

Occasional meal or transportation money.[20] An unusual exception to the "no cash or cash equivalent" rule is the payment of meal money or local transportation fare when an employee is required to work overtime. Such occasions should be infrequent in nature and without any regularity as to occurrence.[21]

Employee-achievement awards. A church may operate a length-of-service or safety-achievement award as a de minimis fringe benefit program utilizing the above rules or it may operate an employee-achievement award program under the provisions of IRC Sections 74 and 274. When an employee-achievement award exceeds the de minimis fringe benefit provisions, it can still be provided as a tax-free award to an employee if it is:

- transferred by the church to an employee for length of service achievement[22] or safety achievement;

- awarded as a part of a meaningful presentation;

- awarded under conditions and circumstances that do not create a significant likelihood of the payment of disguised compensation;

- made up only of items of tangible personal property (ineligible items include cash, gift cards, vacations, meals, lodging, tickets to sporting events/theater events, stocks or other securities); and

- given as a part of an overall program in which the cost of all the employee-achievement awards given to an employee throughout the year does not exceed $400. If the award

---

[20] IRC Section 132(e)(2)
[21] Treas. Reg. Section 1.132-6(d)(2)
[22] IRC Section 274(j)(4)(B) states a length of service may not be awarded in the first five years of employment or more frequently than once every five years.

is part of a "qualified" plan, the total cost limit (including awards under a nonqualifying plan) is $1,600.

Qualified Employee Achievement Award Plan[23]: An employer may create a qualified plan allowing for the higher award limit with two significant limitations:

> › The plan must be a written plan and may not discriminate in favor of highly compensated employees. A plan may be determined to discriminate in favor of highly compensated employees if a review of the actual operations of the plan indicates such discrimination exist.

> › The total awards provided in any one year does not average more than $400 per award. The average is calculated based on the sum of the costs to the employer for all employee-achievement awards/the total number of employee achievement-awards presented. In calculating this average, the church would include all employee-achievement awards, including those with a nominal value awarded under IRC Section 132(e).

Qualified Transportation Fringe*

In general, commuting expenses of an employee may not be provided by the church. The qualified transportation fringe benefit provides the only avenue for churches to pay for commuting expenses. The benefit plan may be wholly funded by the church, or the church may establish a plan funded by the employees' elective deferrals. (See the definition of "elective deferral" in Chapter 8.)

Benefits available include expenses incurred or reimbursed for:

• Transportation in a commuter highway vehicle, furnished by or for the employer, between an employee's residence and place of employment. A commuter highway vehicle seats at least 6 adults besides the driver, spends at least 80 percent of its mileage for commuting, and transports passengers, of which 50 percent are employees of the church;

• Transit passes for any mass transit facilities. The total value between transportation in a commuter highway vehicle and for transit passes may not exceed $260[24] per month; and

• Qualified parking not to exceed $260[25] per month.

---

[23] Prop. Reg. Section 1.274-5
[24] Amount available for 2018. The monthly limits are indexed each year for inflation and should be reviewed on an annual basis.
[25] Amount available for 2018. The monthly limits are indexed each year for inflation and should be reviewed on an annual basis.

Warning: *Effective for expenses incurred after December 31, 2017, a church providing for qualified transportation fringe benefits must now report the expenses associated with the benefits as unrelated business income on Form 990-T and pay income tax at the corporate rate of 21 percent.[26] Churches desiring to avoid filing Form 990-T for this provision should seek professional assistance in restructuring compensation plans before instituting changes in compensation and benefit planning.*

Example 9-15

First Church is in the heart of a large city. Parking available around the church is limited and very expensive. To assist employees, First Church pays for a parking pass for each of its employees. The value of the monthly parking pass is $200. The parking is directly paid each month by the church to the owner of the parking garage. Since the amount paid each month is less than $260, the benefit is a qualified transportation fringe benefit and is not taxable to the employee. First Church is required to file Form 990-T reporting the value of the monthly parking passes as taxable income on the Form 990-T.

Restrictions

Dollar limitations are calculated on a monthly basis and a shortage in one month does not create additional funds to be used in a following month.

Reimbursements for qualified expenses may not be made for expenses not yet incurred.

Transit passes may not be provided for more than three months at a time.

Warning: *There are many methods to provide for benefits under these plans. Some methods may entail restrictions outside the scope of this chapter. This is especially true if the plan allows for employee elective deferrals. Churches should have their plans reviewed by a tax professional to provide assurance that the tax benefits will be maintained under the plan.*

Allowable Recipients

Qualified transportation fringe benefit plans may only be provided to current employees of the church at the time the qualified transportation is provided. A plan may cover any and/or all church employees. A plan may not provide expenses after an employee leaves the church's employment.

Example 9-16

First Church provides metro passes to its employees. The metro passes are issued on the first day of each quarter of the year. Joe receives his metro pass on July 1. On July

---

[26] IRC Section 512(a)(7)

31, he resigns from the church effective August 1. Because of Joe's resignation, one month of the metro pass is a qualified transportation fringe benefit. The value of the other two months is a taxable benefit and must be included on Joe's Form W-2.

On-Premises Athletic Facilities

The value of on-site athletic facilities is not included in an employee's income.

Restrictions

To qualify as a benefit, it is required that the facility:

- Must be located on the church's premises;

- Must be operated by the church; and

- Substantially all of the use of facilities is by the employees, their spouses, and their dependents. Making the facility available to the general public for membership or other uses violates this restriction.

ELAINE'S EXTRA

Expenses associated with on-site athletic facilities should be reportable on Form 990-T just like the transportation costs discussed above. However, a technical glitch in the 2017 Tax Cuts and Jobs Act failed to change another code section as required by the law. The technicality may be corrected by future tax legislation. Churches with these facilities should be aware that potential changes in this area may create a Form 990-T filing requirement.

Allowable Recipients

The benefit may be provided to employees. Employees include:

- Any individual currently employed by the church;

- Any individual formerly employed by the church but has separated from service due to retirement or disability;

- Any widow or widower of the two groups listed above; and

- Any spouse or dependent child of the persons listed above.

Example 9-17

First Church has athletic facilities on its premises. The facilities are only available to the church's employees and their families. In addition to the athletic facilities, First Church employs a trainer to operate the facilities. The trainer is available for personal tips and instruction as to how to use the equipment. Employees may also make personal appointments with the trainer for private training sessions. The value of the athletic facilities is a nontaxable fringe benefit, but the value of the personal trainer sessions must be included in the applicable employee's income.

Warning: *Churches often operate on-premises athletic facilities predominately for the use by church members and the related community. These facilities fail the "use" test of this benefit provision. If the facilities are operated for the general betterment of the community without charge, the use by employees would not be taxable. However, if the facilities are restricted to church members and employees only, or the facilities are provided for a fee, the provision may be taxable if provided free of charge to employees who are not church members.*

ELAINE'S EXTRA

For many reasons, retirement savings is too often ignored by churches and their employees. Providing retirement plans, and encouraging employees to participate in them, should be viewed as a plan for relieving future church congregations from the financial needs that may arise when people in their communities do not have enough retirement and emergency funds to provide for expenses in their later years due to lack of planning in their earlier years.

Qualified Retirement Planning

Many churches operate retirement plans, but few churches realize they may provide planning services to employees as a fringe benefit. Available only to churches with retirement plans, planning services may include information about the plan and service, evaluating an employee's retirement income needs, and the goals necessary to meet those needs.

Restrictions

Qualified retirement planning services may not include tax preparation, accounting, legal, or brokerage services offered by an employer who maintains a qualified employer plan.

The services may not be provided on a discriminatory basis in favor of highly compensated employees. The services must be made available on substantially the same terms to each employee who is normally provided education and information regarding the church's retirement plan.

Allowable Recipients

Retirement planning services may be offered to the church's current employees and their spouses.

Taxable Benefits and Payroll Taxes

Taxable income from any of the benefits above is created if IRS rules are not followed or the benefit provided is more than the amount allowed. Churches may treat the taxable portion of the fringe benefit as paid on December 31 of each year for purposes of reporting income and withholding and depositing taxes.[27] Churches also may elect to treat benefits as paid on a pay period, quarterly, or semi-annually. The election does not have to be the same for all employees. This provision provides a church time to evaluate and value benefits for potential inclusion in income and relieves a church from amending payroll reporting for taxable benefits inadvertently provided earlier in the calendar year.

> **Example 9-18**
>
> First Church provides parking for its business administrator, David, at a nearby parking garage. The value of the parking is $300 per month. As a qualified transportation fringe benefit, $260 of the benefit is tax free. The other $40 of the parking benefit must be included in the business administrator's taxable income. The church elects to treat the taxable portion of the benefit as paid on the last payroll of the tax year. With this pay-roll, the church adds $480 to David's payroll (12 months x $40), so all the applicable taxes may be withheld and paid on the taxable fringe benefit.

CHAPTER 9 KEY POINTS:

- Even common benefits associated with an employment arrangement may have applicable rules that need to be followed.

- Discounts or free services may create taxable income to an employee.

- Commuting benefits may not be provided, except under a qualified transportation fringe benefit program.

- Accounting for the taxes due on taxable fringe benefits may be done at year-end or on another basis as elected by the church.

---

[27] Ann 85-113, 1985-31 IRB 31; IR 85-70, 7/19/85

LIFE-RELATED BENEFITS

Providing employees with more than cash compensation

When church leaders talk about compensation and payroll, they often focus only on cash compensation. But they should also consider compensation that goes beyond cash, which includes fringe benefit plans. This rounds out a compensation package and creates employee loyalty and longevity. Since many church employees work for less than market value, providing these employees with more than a cash compensation package is essential.

In Chapter 9, we discussed *work-related* fringe benefits. In this chapter, we will discuss *life-related* benefits. These address employees' needs *outside the workplace* and include:

- **Healthcare.** Covering medical expenses remains one of the top priorities for all of today's workers—and it is one of the most expensive benefits for employers to provide. There are many options, and while these options offer a variety of benefits, they also create a confusing maze of tax complications.

- **Disability.** Of people ages 18 to 64, 10.4 percent are disabled.[1] Assisting staff members in planning for these potential events may relieve a church's burden of trying to care for an affected staff member, both financially and emotionally, if an event occurs.

- **Life Insurance.** It is estimated that 41 percent of Americans do not have life insurance, and of those who do, roughly one-third of them have only the basic amounts provided through group policies.[2] While not a popular topic of conversation, providing life insurance for staff members may provide the greatest benefit to the church at the time of an unexpected tragedy.

---

[1] 2016 Disability Statistics Annual Report – Rehabilitation Research and Training Center on Disability Statistics and Demographics https://disabilitycompendium.org/sites/default/files/user-uploads/2016_AnnualReport.pdf

[2] https://www.bestliferates.org/blog/2017-life-insurance-statistics-and-facts/

- **Time Off.** Work/life balance is a top priority for workers and one of the most difficult to maintain when working for a church. This is especially true for those who work for and attend the same church. Complicating this subject are little-known tax rules churches generally miss or ignore.

- **Education.** Education costs continue to increase, and providing employees a path to pursue education is a valuable benefit. If carefully navigated, a church can encourage an employee's education and provide a tax-free benefit.   Special plans may also allow a church to provide education to employees' dependents—this is a benefit that is not just limited to employees.

- **Dependent Care.** Childcare costs range from $4,000 to $12,000 per year depending on locale, with even higher rates in some parts of the country. This life cost is a consideration to workers with children, especially infants and toddlers. Exploring methods to assist in this cost to staff can pay big dividends in employee loyalty.

- **Retirement.** Americans sorely lack retirement assets, and studies show that churches and their ministers are not adequately planning for retirement. "A 2015 survey of more than 4,000 pastors nationwide provides a sobering statistic: one in five pastors do not save anything for retirement."[3] Other information indicates that more than 51 percent of Americans aren't actively contributing to employer-sponsored plans and they aren't contributing to other types of retirement plans outside of work either.[4] This information indicates that vehicles for retirement planning are important to both a church's ministers and its lay employees.

To gain employee satisfaction, loyalty, and longevity, churches must provide compensation plans that address various aspects of employees' lives and not just the cash in their paychecks. While a church may not be able to afford to offer all of these benefits, it should attempt to identify the ones it can afford to provide and then work carefully to provide them in a legal- and tax-compliant manner. Resources available on ChurchSalary.com can help a church determine what other congregations of similar size and setting are providing to ministers and staff members, which can be a helpful starting point.

When a church provides these plans in an advantageous manner to the employees and the church, it maximizes the funding it can provide to the plans. Structuring these benefits in

---

[3] *Planning a Pastor's Retirement* http://www.churchlawandtax.com/blog/2017/september/ planning-pastors-retirement.html

[4] *Americans Still Missing the Boat on Retirement Savings* https://www.forbes.com/sites/ kateashford/2018/02/28/retirement-3/#31d0f3b56935

a tax-free arrangement may allow for funding to be obtained from either the church or the employee or a combination. Carefully structured benefit arrangements also maximize employees' perceived value of what is provided and of the church as an employer.

Fringe benefit plans have many intricacies, and this chapter simply introduces the most common types of fringe benefits available for church employees—plus some insights regarding how they work and what potential legal or tax angles leaders should consider before opting to offer them.

> **ELAINE'S EXTRA**
>
> All fringe benefits are taxable unless the church meets the stringent requirements to make them nontaxable. A church should engage an attorney, a CPA, or a benefit specialist to assist it with meeting all of the tax-free requirements. The potential costs to the employee and the church are too significant to have the church skimp on utilizing professionals in creating benefit plans.

Healthcare Benefits

There are a number of methods to provide health benefit plans, which include:

Group health insurance plans

Qualifying group health insurance premiums paid by the church may be provided tax-free for the portion paid by the employer. A qualifying group health insurance policy means that the policy meets all of the requirements of the Affordable Care Act (ACA). Amounts paid by employees must be paid through a Section 125/Cafeteria plan to be paid with pre-tax dollars (see the discussion of these plans in Chapter 8).[5] Premiums paid by employees outside of a Section 125/Cafeteria plan are paid with post-tax dollars by the employees.

Individual health insurance plans

While a church may pay for an employee's individual health insurance premium tax-free,[6] the payment of individual insurance plans creates a health reimbursement plan that violates the ACA requirements. Any such violation subjects a church to a penalty of $100 per day per participant. This penalty must be voluntarily reported to the Internal Revenue Service along with payment of the penalty amount(s) owed.

Plans involving fewer than two participants are not subject to ACA market reforms and can

---

[5] The ACA requires group health insurance to be provided on a basis that does not discriminate in favor of highly compensated employees. Notice 2011 suspended these provisions until after the issuance of guidance defining the nondiscrimination rules. As of this publication, no guidance has been issued.

[6] Notice 2015-17

continue in much the same manner as prior to the passage of the ACA. This includes the reimbursement of premiums for individual health insurance plans.[7]

Insurance for Ancillary Services

Insurance for vision and dental are excluded from ACA requirements. Insurance premiums may be paid by the employer tax-free or they may be paid through a qualifying Section 125/Cafeteria plan.

Section 125/Cafeteria Plan Health Flexible Spending Accounts

Churches offering Section 125/Cafeteria plans may include a provision for employees to establish flexible spending accounts to cover out-of-pocket medical expenses. The flex spending account may be funded through tax-free employer contributions or through the employees' pre-tax salary reduction contributions to the plan. Employee pre-tax salary reduction contributions are limited to $2,650[8] per year. (This amount is indexed each year.)

The flexible spending account may not be used to pay for any individual insurance premiums or medical benefits other than for excluded services, such as vision or dental plans. Allowing flex plans to pay for individual medical insurance policies causes the plan to fail the ACA market reforms and subjects the church to the $100 per day per participant penalty.[9]

Participants in a Section 125 flex spending plan may not also participate in a health savings account offered by the church.

Health Reimbursement Accounts (HRA)

Health reimbursement accounts are employer-funded health plans that reimburse employees for qualified medical expenses up to a fixed dollar, per year, tax-free. Prior to the ACA, these plans could cover a variety of expenses. However, to comply with ACA requirements, the HRA must be integrated with a qualifying group health plan. Additionally, the HRA may only cover medical expenses of the persons participating in the integrated group health plan.

Example 10-1

First Church offers a group health insurance plan for its employees. Joe, a full-time employee, opts to enter the group health plan for himself. His spouse and children are covered under his spouse's group health insurance plan. First Church also provides an HRA available to reimburse up to $5,000 of medical expenses not covered by the group health plan. Joe may submit medical expenses for himself to the HRA for reimburse-

---

[7] Notice 2015-87 and Notice 2013-54
[8] Amount allowable in 2018
[9] Notice 2015-87

ment, but he may not submit his spouse's medical expenses, since she is not covered by First Church's group health insurance.

An HRA may not reimburse for individual health insurance policy premiums. Reimbursing individual health insurance premiums does not comply with ACA market reforms and the plan is subject to the $100 per day per participant penalty. The HRA may reimburse for individual plan premiums for excluded benefits, such as dental or vision benefits.

Qualified Small Employer HRA (QSEHRA)

Recognizing the above rules created unintended effects on small employers, Congress created a special HRA plan for small employers to utilize for reimbursing individual health insurance premiums. This plan is called the Qualified Small Employer HRA (QSEHRA). A church may qualify for a QSEHRA if it has less than 50 full-time equivalent employees. A QSEHRA requires a written plan document defining the plan and containing all the mandatory requirements of the plan. Requirements of QSEHRA are as follows:

- All eligible employees must be offered the plan;

- Employees must provide proof of having minimum essential health coverage;

- The employer may not offer group health insurance;

- The employer must fully fund (100 percent) the plan;

- Written notice must be provided to employees;

- The maximum reimbursement is $5,050 for employee-only coverage and $10,250 for family coverage (amounts may be indexed annually).

The QSEHRA is the only method available for a church to reimburse an employee's individual health insurance premiums. However, it may not be used to reimburse the premium for a policy obtained through an insurance exchange.

Warning: *The QSEHRA is only available when a church does not offer a group health insur-*

> **ELAINE'S EXTRA**
>
> After Congress passed the QSEHRA, many churches were incorrectly informed that the payment of individual health insurance premiums was once again allowed. This is far from true. The QSEHRA has many requirements and most small churches have not taken steps to adopt the proper plan, meaning they are still in violation of ACA requirements and subject to related penalties.

ance plan. Many denominational plans are available to member churches even if the member church does not use the plan or has only a few employees using the plan. In these instances, it may be construed that the member church participates in a group plan and is not eligible to operate the QSEHRA.

Health Savings Accounts (HSA)

To allow employees and employers to utilize a lower-cost option for health insurance, Congress created the health savings accounts (HSA) to work with health insurance plans which carry higher deductible limits.

A HSA is an account set up with a qualified trustee to reimburse certain medical expenses. An HSA must be established by an individual covered by a high deductible health plan (HDHP), as defined by the IRS. For 2018, an HDHP is defined as:

	Self-Only Coverage	Family Coverage
Minimum annual deductible	$1,350	$2,700
Maximum annual deductible and other out-of-pocket expenses within the network, if the plan uses network providers	$6,650	$13,300

Other health coverage may not be available except for coverages for accidents, disability, dental, vision, and long-term care. Contributions to the plan may be made:

- Directly by an individual and deducted on his individual tax return;

- Directly by an employer and not included in the employee's income; or

- An employee may also make contributions through payroll deduction. However, under the concepts discussed in Chapter 8, any contributions coming through an employee's paycheck must be made through an employer's Section 125/Cafeteria plan to be a pre-tax contribution. Employees participating in flexible spending accounts provided by the plan are prohibited from contributing to a health savings account.

Annual contributions are limited and may be indexed each year by the IRS. For 2018, contribution limits are $3,450 for individual coverage and $6,900 for family coverage.

Healthcare Costs Sharing Plans

The Christian community has created its own unique provision for healthcare costs through the creation of healthcare costs sharing plans. Organizations offering these plans are commonly tax-exempt entities and are not insurance companies. The product offered is not insurance, and benefits are not guaranteed to the participants. Participants in these programs are exempt from the ACA's individual mandate (the mandate is repealed as of December 31, 2018).

Churches may encounter these arrangements through a staff member's participation in the plan. Reimbursement of the plan participation costs carries all of the same consequences as reimbursing individual health insurance plans and should be avoided. Churches desiring to use these arrangements to provide group health coverage to their employees must treat the coverage as the creation of a self-insured plan. Since these plans have many individual requirements, churches should seek professional guidance to create a plan that both complies with federal tax law and with the ACA.

The costs to participate in these plans do not qualify as a medical expense and may not be reimbursed through a Section 125/Cafeteria plan's flexible spending plan, a HSA, or a HRA. The cost of participation is also not deductible by an individual on his or her personal tax return. If the church pays the employee's cost to participate in the plan, those payments must be included in the employee's taxable income, unless the church has incorporated the payments into a nondiscriminatory self-insured health plan.

Disability Insurance

Disability insurance is the most overlooked life benefit, yet one of the most needed life benefits. It is estimated that 1 in 10 Americans become disabled prior to retirement. Therefore, churches should consider this benefit. This is especially true for employees with little or no retirement assets.

Tax consequences of providing disability insurance as a benefit are different from other types of "health" plans. Amounts received through an accident or health plan are includible in income if they are attribut-

ELAINE'S EXTRA

The sudden incapacitation of a church's senior minister can devastate a congregation. Leaders naturally will want to provide the minister with a form of continued support, even though he or she may not be able to perform services. Rules regarding reasonable compensation, though, prohibit the church from providing support without a corresponding return of services (see Chapter 3). A good disability policy is a better way for a church to provide for its ministers if they ever become suddenly disabled or incapacitated.

able to amounts paid by the employer.[10] An exception applies to amounts received for the reimbursement of medical expenses. (This is the provision allowing regular proceeds from health insurance policies to avoid taxation.) Since the proceeds from disability insurance are not used for the reimbursement of medical expenses, the proceeds are subject to the general rules of taxation.

If an employee pays tax on the premiums for the disability income policy, then the employee will not have to pay tax on the distributions under the policy.[11] If the premiums are not taxed to the employee, the policy distributions will be taxable to the recipient. Churches should offer access to disability policies even if they do not contribute to the premiums. If the church contributes to the premiums, it should consider making the amounts paid for the premiums an addition to taxable income.

Example 10-2

First Church purchases both short-term and long-term disability policies for each of its ministers and short-term disability policies for all of its other full-time staff members. The church has never included the premiums in any of its employees' taxable income. Sue, a full-time employee, has surgery and is out of work for 12 weeks. Her short-term disability policy pays her $10,000 during her medical leave. Since the policy premiums were never included on her Form W-2, Sue must include the $10,000 on her Form 1040 as taxable income.

Example 10-3

Same facts as in Example 10-2, except First Church includes the value of the premium in each employees' income each year. Pastor Joe has an auto accident resulting in a severe disability. Pastor Joe's long-term disability policy will pay him $50,000 per year if he is disabled. Because the value of the premium was included in Pastor Joe's income each year by the church, Pastor Joe need not include the $50,000 on his Form 1040 each year.

Churches with limited paid leave time may provide disability insurance to assist with short-term leaves, such as maternity leaves or surgery recovery time. Long-term disability policies provide living expenses if an employee could not continue his or her duties for a substantial period of time or permanently.

Life Insurance

Most American families are not prepared for a tragedy that removes the primary wage earner

---

[10]   IRC Section 105(a)
[11]   IRS Private Letter Ruling 200146010, 200146011, 200146012

from the household. This often includes those who work for churches. Even if the person lost to the unexpected event is a spouse not in the work force, a financial burden is created for the family. Often, the financial burden created when a family loses a loved one is placed on the church, who feels a responsibility to assist during this time of unexpected need. This dynamic can be avoided through life insurance. While life insurance is not the most popular of benefits, it is a need for most families. Life insurance may be provided to employees through two plans:

- **Group Plans.** Group-term life insurance is a policy carried by the church covering a group of employees. Coverage may be provided tax-free by the church for up to $50,000 on the employee's life and up to $2,000 of coverage for his or her spouse and dependents. Coverage in excess of $50,000 is valued using the IRS Premium Table in IRS Publication 15-B.

A group-term plan is a plan that:

  › Provides a general death benefit that isn't included in income;

  › Is provided to a group of employees (if the group is less than 10 employees, the group must meet special rules to still qualify);

  › Provides for an amount of insurance to each employee based on a formula that prevents individual selection. Factors to select coverage may include age, years of service, pay, or position; and,

  › Is directly or indirectly provided by the employer.

- **Individual-Term Life Plans.** Coverage provided to just one or more specific employees, not considered as group coverage, is taxable based on the cost of the premiums.

- **Whole-Life Insurance Plans.** Whole-life insurance has many varying options on structure of ownership and benefits. Outside of the policy being solely used to provide an investment for the church and key-man life insurance, using a whole-life policy will create a taxable benefit to an employee. Churches utilizing whole-life policies should consult with a tax professional to determine the tax effects of the policy to the employee, including a determination on whether the use of the policy creates a nonqualified deferred compensation plan under IRC Section 409A. (See discussion under "Retirement Plans" later in this chapter for more information on nonqualified deferred compensation plans.)

Example 10-4

First Church provides a $1 million term life policy on its senior pastor. Of the $1 million proceeds, $500,000 of the proceeds are payable to the church and $500,000 of the proceeds are payable to the pastor's wife. The policy is not a part of a group-term life insurance plan. Of the total annual premium paid, half must be included as taxable income on the pastor's Form W-2.

Example 10-5

First Church provides a group-term life insurance for its employees. Tom is a full-time employee of the church and is provided $200,000 of coverage (based on 2 times Tom's annual salary). The church must calculate the value of the coverage in excess of $50,000 of coverage ($150,000). According to Publication 15-B, the $150,000 of coverage works out to $270 per year in taxable income. The $270 is included in Boxes 1, 3, and 5, since Tom is not a minister, and in Box 12 with a code of "C."

Vacation and Other Leave Plans

Paid time off is a common and valuable benefit. For many employees, time off is a major factor in job satisfaction. While vacation or other leave plans are common, most employers, including churches, do not realize that some arrangements may create adverse tax consequences.

Paid time off plans consisting of "use it or lose it" policies rarely create an adverse tax consequence. Plans allowing for the accrual of unused time to future years, or plans allowing for the cashing out of unused time, easily can run afoul of tax rules. These plans can become taxable to an employee in the year earned rather than the year the time off is used or is cashed out.

Paid time off plans allowing for future benefits attributable to unused time may be taxable either through applying the constructive receipt doctrine or the rules related to nonqualified deferred compensation plans. The constructive receipt doctrine states that if an employee can have access to income, then the employee is taxed when the income is *available* to him or her, rather than *received* by him or her. Closely related to this concept are nonqualified deferred compensation plans where employees can take income earned in one year and defer its receipt, and taxation, to a later tax year.

A vacation or leave plan does not run afoul of these concepts if it is a bona fide vacation, sick leave, or compensatory time off plan.[12] Any plan outside of the basic "use it or lose it" basis must be reviewed to determine if it is a "bona fide" plan. This is especially true if the plan allows any benefits earned in one tax year to be utilized or cashed out in a later tax year.

To be a bona fide plan, the following factors should be considered:

- Whether the amount of leave provided could reasonably be expected to be used in the normal course of the year by an employee (before the employee ceases to provide services to the eligible employer), absent unusual circumstances, to exchange unused accumulated leave for cash or other benefits (including nontaxable benefits and the use of leave to postpone the date of voluntary termination of employment). Plans allowing for an extraordinary accrual of time off that cannot be reasonably utilized by an employee in a year may indicate the plan's intent is to defer compensation. (If all of this sounds ambiguous, it is—and if your church faces such a situation, it likely needs professional help);

- The applicable restraints (if any) on the ability to accumulate unused leave and carry it forward to later years if the accumulated leave may be exchanged for cash or other benefits. Plans allowing for unlimited accruals of unused hours are less likely to be bona fide plans;

- The amount and frequency of any in-service distributions of cash or other benefits offered in exchange for accumulated and unused leave. If a plan allows an employee to ask for unused time to be converted to cash at any time at the discretion of the employee, the benefits under the plan will be taxable at the point the employee earns them;

- Whether any payment of unused leave is made promptly upon the end of an employment arrangement (or is instead paid over a period from the end of the employment). A common component is to provide a cash-out at termination (voluntary and/or involuntary). (Some state laws require employers to pay accrued vacation pay at termination.) However, if termination is the triggering factor, then it may not be deferred to later times at the election of the employee. There may be exceptions for plans providing for a conversion of unused time to a contribution to a qualified retirement plan and taxing the benefits when they are distributed from the qualified retirement plan; and,

---

12 IRC Section 409A(d)(1)(B)

- Whether the program (or a particular feature of the program) is available only to a limited number of employees.[13] Programs available to a small group of key employees take on the appearance of a deferred compensation plan and not a bona fide leave plan.

Example 10-6

First Church allows its ministers to accumulate all unused vacation time on an ongoing basis and without limitation from year to year. When a minister's employment with the church ends, he or she may select to receive the value of all unused time, either as one lump sum or to be paid out over 10 years. No other employees, except the ministers, are granted this plan. First Church's plan does not qualify as a bona fide vacation plan. The plan does not allow for any restrictions on the time accrued; it is provided to a select group of key individuals; and it allows for a greater deferral after the end of the minister's employment arrangement with the church.

Educational Plans

Educational Assistance Plans

Churches often desire to provide for an employee's additional education but fail to recognize the limitations associated with providing educational benefits to employees. When education qualifies as continuing education required to maintain an employee's position, the church is not limited in its assistance. (Continuing education is discussed in Chapter 9, and see page 169 for a comparison of continuing education plans and educational assistance plans.) However, when education cannot meet the qualifications of continuing education, then the church is limited to the rules governing educational assistance under IRC Section 127. Benefits paid outside of a Section 127 plan must be included in an employee's taxable income.

To qualify as an educational assistance plan, the plan must:

- Be provided through a written plan document that is a separate document from an employee handbook. The plan should be individually provided or explained to the employees, and the employees should acknowledge receipt of the plan;

- Limit benefits to $5,250 per year for tuition, fees, and books for college and university classes, including graduate classes;

- Not provide for:

  › Any expenses, except tools, that may be retained after the course;

---

[13] Prop. Treas. Reg. Section 1.475-111(f)(1) provides guidance on the definition of a "bona fide" vacation leave plan that is also utilized for purposes of IRC Section 409A.

> Meals, lodging, or transportation; or

> Education involving sports, games, or hobbies.

• Not discriminate in favor of highly compensated employees.

> Highly compensated is defined as compensation[14] of $120,000 or more in a year. This amount may be indexed from year to year.

Additionally, the plan may be provided to a class of employees if the classification is established under a reasonable and objective set of business criteria. A classification is not reasonable if it has the same effect of naming specific employees due to its narrowness.

Example 10-7

First Church agrees to pay for the doctoral program expenses for its senior pastor. The church does not pay for any other educational expenses for other employees. The expenses for the doctoral program qualify the senior pastor for a new job and are not required for him to maintain his position at First Church. Therefore, the expenses do not qualify as continuing education expenses.[15] Since the church has no educational assistance plan available to its employees, the expenses cannot be paid through an educational assistance plan. All amounts paid for the pastor's doctoral program must be included on the pastor's Form W-2 as additional compensation.

Tuition-Reduction Plans

Many churches operate schools. While some churches may operate post-secondary programs, the majority of church-operated schools encompass pre-K through 12th grade programs. The National Center for Education Statistics states that there were more than 5 million students enrolled in private schools for the 2015-2016 school year.[16] Of the 34,576 private schools reported in the 2015-2016 school year, 67 percent maintained a religious affiliation.[17]

Tuition-reduction plans allow "schools" to provide employees, their spouses, and their dependents with a reduction in tuition charges in a tax-free manner. To qualify, the tuition reduction plan must:

• Provide benefits to employees of the school. This restricts eligible employees to those

---

[14] Compensation is defined by IRC Code Section 415(c). It generally is compensation reported in Box 1 of Form W-2 with amounts for elective deferrals under IRC Code Sections 402(g)(3), 125, 132(f)(4) and/or 457 added back into the amount.

[15] Czarnecki, Jr. v. U.S., Ct Fed Cl, 120 AFTR 2d 2017-6173, 10/13/2017

[16] https://nces.ed.gov/programs/digest/d16/tables/dt16_205.10.asp?current=yes

[17] https://nces.ed.gov/surveys/pss/tables/table_2015_04.asp

associated with the school's operations and excludes employees wholly dedicated to the church's operations; and

- Not provide benefits in a manner that discriminates in favor of highly compensated employees.[18] The benefits may be provided at different levels for different classes of individuals, so long as the classification does not result in a discriminatory classification.[19]

Dependent Care Plan

In January 2018, the US Bureau of Labor Statistics reported 96.8 million full-time employees and 16.2 million part-time employees between the ages of 20 and 54.[20] The Center for American Progress reports that less than 1 in 3 children today have a full-time stay-at-home parent.[21] As employers, churches must recognize that many of their pastors and employees are dealing with dependent care outside the home. Depending on the income of the family, the cost of dependent care may range from 10 percent to 49 percent of the family's income.[22]

> **ELAINE'S EXTRA**
> While it is clear that a school offering classes for 1st through 12th grades qualifies as a school, the classification is less clear for programs offering care and classes for infants through K-5. If a church only operates a preschool program, it should consult with a professional to determine if it is operating a "school" or a "daycare" for purposes of determining if the benefit plan offered is a tuition reduction plan under IRC Section 117 or a dependent care plan under IRC Section 129.

Churches can assist in this cost, but they must do so within the confines of the requirements for dependent care plans. Churches may do one of the following options:

Option 1: Churches may allow staff members to utilize onsite facilities. This is a popular method for churches operating daycare centers or preschools. Benefits may be provided through fee discounts for employees;

Option 2: Out of the church's funds, it may opt to reimburse staff members for out-of-pocket daycare costs; or

---

[18] Highly compensated is determined in reference to IRC Section 414(q)
[19] IRC Section 117(d)
[20] https://www.bls.gov/cps/cpsaat08.htm U.S. Department of Labor Bureau of Labor Statistics
[21] Center for American Progress https://www.americanprogress.org/issues/economy/news/2012/08/16/11978/fact-sheet-child-care/
[22] Center for American Progress https://www.americanprogress.org/issues/economy/news/2012/08/16/11978/fact-sheet-child-care/

Option 3: Churches may allow staff members to fund a dependent care plan through a salary reduction agreement.

While these three avenues are available to the church, all three require the establishment of a qualifying dependent care plan. To qualify, the dependent care plan must:

- Be defined through a separate written plan of the church;

- Not discriminate in favor of highly compensated employees;

- Provide participants with a written statement showing amounts paid under the plan (fulfilled by indicating this amount in Box 10 on Form W-2); and

- Limit tax-free benefits to $5,000 per year (greater benefits may be provided, but are not tax-free).

Example 10-8

First Church operates a childcare center. The church allows all full-time church employees a 50-percent discount on the fees charged by the childcare center. Diane is a full-time church member and sends her two-year-old to the center. Her employee discount is $110 per week. For the year, the total discount received through the plan is $5,720. Of the discount, $5,000 may be omitted from Diane's taxable income and $720 must be included as taxable income in Boxes 1, 3, and 5 of her Form W-2. Additionally, the entire $5,720 must be reported in Box 10 on her Form W-2.

Retirement Plans

According to the US Social Security Administration, a man reaching 65 today can expect to live until 84 and a woman can expect to live until 86. However, among 65-year-olds living today, about 1 in 4 will live past the age of 90.[23] This is a remarkable development: for most of the past century, if a person made it to 65, they had reached their expected life span.

The Social Security system was created during a time when the majority of Americans never

---

[23] https://www.ssa.gov/planners/lifeexpectancy.html

ELAINE'S EXTRA

Churches should provide retirement savings accounts to employees and encourage employees to save. Even small contributions to plans can provide for needed benefits in the future. For ministers filing Form 4361 (opting out of self-employment tax), it is imperative that both the church and the minister actively work to provide replacements for the benefits traditionally offered by the Social Security Administration, especially retirement benefits.

reached retirement age. The system was never meant to support people averaging 20 or more years of life after reaching their retirement ages. As a result, retirement planning today is as vital a benefit program as providing health benefit plans for employees. The general goal of retirement plans is to take funds available today, find a method to save them for the future, and defer the income tax burden on the invested funds and their earnings to the time the funds are utilized. There are several options. Often, churches also are granted greater leniency in providing retirement benefits than most other employers, something that should be noted when evaluating these options.

The options include:

- Qualified plans, including 401(k) plans;

- Tax-sheltered annuity plans or 403(b) plans;

- Simplified plans utilizing Individual Retirement Accounts (IRAs); and

- Nonqualified deferred compensation plans, including "rabbi trusts."

It is beyond the scope of this book to provide all the information pertinent to any retirement plan. The following summary briefly describes the available options, along with the key tax aspects affecting compensation and payroll, which should allow a church to begin determining the best one (or ones) to further pursue.

Qualified Retirement Plans

Qualified retirement plans allow employees to save funds for the future without currently paying income tax on the funds. For most of these plans, the taxation of the funds is deferred until the funds are removed from the plan by the participant. Qualified plans include defined benefit plans and defined contribution plans.

Defined Benefit Plans

Contributions to a defined benefit plan are based on a set amount the participant wants to receive in the future (the target benefit). These plans are rarely utilized in today's retirement world. They include more risk to the employer than defined contribution plans.

Defined Contribution Plans

In a defined contribution plan, contributions are given to the plan today and the balance is determined by the investments' performance over the years. Plans commonly known as 401(k) plans and 403(b) plans are both types of defined contribution plans.

No matter the plan a church operates—a defined benefit plan, a 401(k) plan, or a 403(b) plan—it must be diligent to operate the plan in compliance with legal requirements. To stay in compliance, several key aspects of a plan should be regularly reviewed. (Since defined benefit plans are uncommon for churches, the remainder of the discussion will center on defined contribution plans.)

Basic Operating Rules for Qualified Retirement Plans

Whether a defined benefit plan or a defined contribution plan, all qualified retirement plans have specific operating rules:

Plan Documents

A detailed written document is required for qualified retirement plans. Failure to have the proper plan documentation disqualifies the plan, and all contributions to the plan will be taxable on a current basis. For many years, 403(b) plans did not require a plan document, but these rules changed several years ago. Many churches do not realize the need for a plan document.

Example 10-9

Pastor Joe recently joined the staff at First Church. In establishing his compensation package, he requested the church withhold $100 per paycheck and remit it to his 403(b) account at a brokerage house. First Church has no retirement plan but agrees to Pastor Joe's request. Because First Church does not have a 403(b) plan, the $100-per-paycheck contributions by Pastor Joe are a post-tax contribution to the account.

Example 10-10

Same facts as in Example 10-9, except First Church is a part of a denomination with a denominational pension board. Pastor Joe has an account with the denominational 403(b) plan and requests his contributions go to his account. First Church is contributing to a valid 403(b) plan operated by the denomination and the amounts withheld and remitted to this account are legitimate 403(b) contributions, meaning the contributions may be made on a pre-tax basis.

Plan Adoption Agreements

Any retirement plan can be lengthy and complicated. A plan adoption agreement is used by denominations or churches when selecting between different operating options for the plan. Options may exist on how employee eligibility is defined, what compensation is considered for calculating contributions, and how employer contributions will be vested to the participant's ownership. Details like these are set through the plan adoption agreement, which is a primary reason why they should be carefully completed and maintained

ELAINE'S EXTRA

It is important to know the definition of "compensation" for calculating plan contributions. For example, are bonuses included or just base compensation? Compensation should be defined by the plan document. If a church uses a different definition for compensation than the plan document requires, the church could over- or under-contribute to the plan.

by the employer. In essence, these agreements determine how a plan should be operated.

The plan adoption agreement should be reviewed annually to determine compliance with the plan's definitions of compensation and contributions.

Contributions Limits

Contributions to qualified plans are limited by two avenues. A plan document will define the contribution to the plan, and the federal tax code will define the maximum contribution to a plan (normally these limitations are also included in the plan). These calculations may or may not be equal or based on the same calculation. Contribution limits exist for both tax-free salary reduction elective deferrals made by employees and nonelective contributions made by the church. There are also provisions for making additional contributions in certain circumstances.

Total contributions made by the employee and by the church are subject to strict limitations based on the employee's compensation and on overall dollar limits issued each year by the IRS. Understanding the maximum limitation amounts is key since excess contributions can disqualify a plan. Catch-up contributions further complicate calculations of maximum contribution limits of the plan.

Plans might allow for special catch-up elections for persons over the age of 50. Section 403(b) plans may allow for catch-up contributions based on age or years of service. These calculations are provided through the law but also must be provided in plan documents. The catch-up calculations must be reviewed annually for compliance.

For churches, a minister's housing allowance and/or parsonage valuation creates unusual complications in calculating contribution limits. This nontaxable income may not be used in the technical legal calculation of the maximum contribution that may be made to a qualified plan. However, many churches will include the amount in their plan contribution limit calculation. The housing allowance may be used in the plan limit calculation, unless its use creates a greater contribution than allowed by law. Where the legal limits exceed the plan limits, the plan must provide that the legal limits will govern the final annual addition to the plan.

Example 10-11

First Church operates a 403(b) plan and contributes 10 percent of compensation to the plan for all ministers. For ministers, the church's plan states that any housing allowance paid to a minister will be added to the amount reported in Box 1 of the Form W-2 to determine the compensation for the year. Pastor Joe receives a total of $50,000 between salary and housing allowance. However, the majority of Pastor Joe's income is designated as housing and Box 1 on Pastor Joe's Form W-2 only reports $4,000. The plan calls for a $5,000 contribution, but federal tax law limits the contribution to 100 percent of the amount in box 1 or taxable income. Therefore, the church must limit its contribution to $4,000. If the plan document is written correctly, the plan will allow for the contribution to be the lower of the calculated limits or the legal limit.

Churches may inadvertently make contributions in amounts less than called for by the plan documents. In these cases, the church must make up the amounts, plus an earnings factor defined by the US Department of Labor. The plan may also have to undergo a voluntary correction process with the Department of Labor or the IRS.

> ## ELAINE'S EXTRA
>
> Many companies and investment firms offer prototype plans for qualified retirement plans. Prototype plans will be written for the general employer and not for a church employer. If used without an appropriate review, a church may end up with requirements that are unintended, such as mandatory nondiscrimination requirements. The majority of prototype plans include ERISA provisions not generally applicable to a church. Once the plan document is signed, it is binding on the church. Further, such plans cannot designate a housing allowance when distributing benefits.

Access to Funds

Restrictions exist on when funds may be withdrawn from the plans. There may be both age requirements on withdrawals and separation from service requirements. Certain withdrawals may also be allowed in cases of defined hardships. Accessing funds outside the prescribed limits may cause penalties assessed to the participant/employee.

Nondiscrimination Rules

Plans may be subjected to nondiscrimination rules and limit churches from making contributions to only a select few employees. Generally, churches are granted greater leniency in the nondiscrimination rules for 403(b) plans. This lenience is not available in 401(k) plans. These leniency rules are the primary reason the 403(b) plan is the favorite among churches. These special rules for 403(b) plans allow a church to limit contributions for only a select group of employees.

ERISA and the Church

ERISA refers to a specific set of rules applicable to many employer benefit plans through the Employee Retirement Income Security Act of 1974. Church plans are exempt from most ERISA provisions and are free from its restrictions, regulations, and requirements.

A church plan is a plan established and maintained by a church or by a convention or association of churches exempt under IRC Section 501 for the benefit of its employees. While an uncommon occurrence, a church may elect to be subject to the requirement of ERISA. Once a church elects ERISA application to one of its benefit plans, it is not easily changed or undone. Application of ERISA to a church's retirement plan can be detrimental and costly, so a church should consult with qualified legal and tax counsel before doing so.

Remitting Contributions to a Plan

For the church, the payroll department must confirm amounts to be withheld from the employees' pay as elective deferrals for contributions to the plan. These amounts must be properly withheld and reported to accounting. Accounting must assure that all amounts withheld from employees are matched, if required by the plan, and timely remitted to the proper investment funds or trust accounts. The Department of Labor has determined that "timely remitted" is as soon as possible, but **absolutely not** later than within 15 days. If the DOL determines that a reasonable time is the next day, then this time frame is enforced. However, for employers with fewer than 100 participants in the plan, a safe harbor of 7 days is allowed. Funds remitted within 7 days will not face scrutiny for being "timely remitted."

Qualified Retirement Plans and the Minister

Benefits paid to participants are taxed for federal income tax at the time of distribution. For plans offering a "Roth" feature (i.e., a feature allowing for contributions to the plans to be made with after-tax dollars instead of pre-tax dollars), all or a portion of the distributions may be tax-free to the participant. Distributions from qualified retirement plans are not subject to self-employment tax.

Certain plans operated as church plans through denominational pension boards may designate a portion of the distributions as a minister's housing allowance. For churches using independent prototype plans of investments companies or other for-profit agencies, there is not a provision to designate a portion of the payments as housing allowance to the retired minister. However, a church plan may not designate a retirement distribution as housing allowance if the distribution is not paid to a minister. Therefore, retirement distributions paid to surviving spouses are not eligible to be designated as housing allowance.

Retirement Options Using IRAs

Combining the concepts of an employer-provided plan and an IRA, Congress created two easy ways for employers to provide a retirement plan. Both types of plans have strict rules to create plans requiring little administrative effort and/or costs. While these plans are not popular with churches, due to the extensive definition of "eligible employee," churches should know of them to avoid accidentally utilizing an IRA outside of these plans. More information on these plans is provided in IRS Publication 590.

Simplified Employee Pension Plan/SEP-IRA

The Simplified Employee Pension (SEP), or the SEP-IRA, is a specific plan funded 100 percent by employer contributions. The plan utilizes IRAs as the funding vehicle. The SEP:

- Is available to any size of church;

- Is easily established by adopting Form 5305-SEP;

- Has no filing requirement for any type of employer;

- Is funded solely by employer contributions to IRAs established by the employees. Employees may not contribute to the plan;

> **ELAINE'S EXTRA**
>
> The SEP-IRA and SIMPLE IRA are the only methods a church may use to contribute to an employee's IRA on a tax-free basis. Contributions to an employee's IRA outside of these plans represent taxable income to the employee and must be included in Box 1 of Form W-2. Employees may be eligible to take a deduction for the contribution to the IRA on their personal tax returns.

- Is available to all eligible employees who are at least 21 years of age and have performed services for the church 3 out of the last immediately 5 preceding years;

- Is funded through contributions on behalf of all eligible employees of the same percentage of compensation, not to exceed 25 percent of the employee's compensation; and

- Is 100 percent vested immediately to the employees.

SIMPLE IRA

Another option available for simplified retirement planning using the IRA funding mechanism is the SIMPLE IRA. The SIMPLE IRA:

- Is for employers with fewer than 100 employees;

- May be adopted by filing Form 5304-SIMPLE;

- Must be available to any employee receiving at least $5,000 in compensation in any 2 preceding years and is expected to receive $5,000 for the current calendar year;

- Is funded through employees' salary reduction contributions, employer-matching contributions, or employer-nonelective contributions;

- Limits employee contributions through salary reduction agreements to $12,500 during the year for 2018 (the amount may be indexed to a higher amount from year to year);

- Requires employer contributions to be either an employer matching of 3 percent (a lesser percent may be elected under special circumstances) for employees participating in the salary reductions agreements or a nonelective contribution of 2 percent of compensation for all eligible employees.

Nonqualified Deferred Compensation Plans

If a church pays income to an employee in any year after the year in which it was earned, and the payments are outside a qualified retirement plan, then the church is participating in a nonqualified deferred compensation plan.

For many years, nonqualified deferred compensation plans operated with few rules. There are no limits on the amounts to be contributed to the plans and no nondiscrimination requirements, so the plans were excellent avenues for planning for retirement benefits for key executive employees. However, Congress changed the rules in 2004 with the creation of IRC Section 409A. Nonqualified deferred compensation plans must comply with the three primary requirements of IRC Section 409A to avoid current taxation of the funds, higher interest rates on any underpayment of federal income tax based on the current taxation of the funds, and a 20 percent additional tax on the funds.

Nonqualified deferred compensation plans must adhere to the rules of IRC Section 409A in three areas:

1. Distributions from the plans may only occur at set instances that are predefined in the plan and are defined when the deferral of income into the plan is accomplished;

2. Acceleration of benefits is only allowed under the plan based on what is acceptable under IRS regulations; and

3. Amounts to be deferred into plans by the participant must be elected by the last day of the calendar year preceding the year the compensation is earned by the participant. For the first year of eligibility for the plan, the election is made within 30 days of when the participant becomes eligible for the plan. Future elections to delay the timing of distributions under the plan may be made only under specific circumstances.

For nonqualified deferred compensation arrangements not meeting the restriction of Section 409A, the income must be includible in the year earned or in the year it is no longer subject to a substantial risk of forfeiture.

Analyzing nonqualified deferred compensation plans and applying Section 409A is difficult and should be accomplished by a professional familiar with the purposes and requirements of the law. A church's interest is best protected by understanding the arrangements that may be affected by Section 409A and seeking professional assistance in creating or utilizing these arrangements. If a compensation arrangement calls for a payment—one that is earned in one year, and to be paid later than two and a half months after the next calendar year was begun—the arrangement should be reviewed for applying Section 409A. Common areas where arrangements should be reviewed by a professional familiar with the rules of Section 409A include:

Severance Arrangements

While there are exceptions for certain severance arrangements due to involuntary separation from service, other severance arrangements may not comply with the Section 409A rules.

Split Dollar Life Insurance Arrangements

Any time a split dollar life insurance policy is utilized in conjunction with the compensation arrangement of a key staff member, the arrangement should be reviewed by a professional to determine any current income tax issues arising from the insurance component and any deferred compensation issues arising from the ultimate use of the policy proceeds.

Vacation and Time-Off Policies Arrangements

Vacation and time-off policies that provide for the accumulation of benefits, especially those provid-

ELAINE'S EXTRA

Any church either considering or already committed to paying a pastor after retirement out of the church's general assets should seek counsel. Many of these agreements jeopardize the church's tax-exempt status and/or create a serious tax consequence to the pastor. Once an agreement is finalized, the church may have to choose between breaking federal tax law or breaking the contract with the minister.

ing for a future cash payout, should be reviewed considering the deferred compensation rules. See previous discussion on this subject in this chapter.

Rabbi Trusts

If the church creates a trust to hold contributions to a nonqualified deferred compensation plan, these plans are classified as "rabbi trusts" because the IRS first approved them for use in connection with a rabbi's employment by a temple. Rabbi trusts have many complex requirements and require frequent legal reviews to assure compliance with the laws. Rabbi trust arrangements were approved by the IRS 20 years prior to the creation of IRC Section 409A. Entering into a rabbi trust arrangement requires the arrangement to be reviewed from the perspective of Section 409A.

Continued Payments Upon Retirement

It is not uncommon for churches to make up for a lack of retirement planning by contracting with a retiring pastor to make payments to him or his widow for the rest of their lives. These payment arrangements present potentially dangerous arrangements for both the church and the pastor due to the Section 409A rules and the rules governing excess benefit transactions discussed in Chapter 2. These promises of future pay should never be finalized without a review of the arrangement, including these two key areas of tax law.

Retirement Gifts

A similar concern should be raised in preparing to make a large gift to a retiring pastor. IRC Section 102 requires the gift to the retiring pastor be included in his taxable income. IRC Section 4958 requires the gift to be reasonable compensation for services rendered by the pastor. If the gift creates unreasonable compensation in the year of the gift, it is common to create a foundation for the gift, based on prior years' compensation paid being less than reasonable. Does catching up compensation from prior years create a deferral of income subject to Section 409A? It is possible and therefore, any plans for a retirement gift should be reviewed by a professional to ensure that the method for raising the funds for the gift create no legal issues for the church and/or the donor and the payment of the gift creates no excess benefit transaction or a taxation and penalty under Section 409A.

Nonqualified Retirement Plans and the Minister

Benefits paid to participants are taxed for federal income tax during distribution. Unlike qualified retirement plans, distributions from nonqualified retirement plans are generally subject to all employment taxes. However, all amounts received by a minister from a church plan, after a minister retires, are excluded from the definition of self-employment income and are not subject to self-employment tax.[24]

---

[24] IRC Section 1402(a)(8)

Since nonqualified deferred compensation plans are plans directly created and operated by a church, the plans should qualify as "church" plans. A church plan can designate a portion of the distributions to a minister as housing allowance. However, a church plan may not designate a retirement distribution as housing allowance if the distribution is not paid to a minister. Therefore, retirement distributions paid to surviving spouses are not eligible to be designated as housing allowance.

CHAPTER 10 KEY POINTS:

- Life happens, and it affects the effectiveness of a church's operations. Caring for staff members is a critical role for the church but requires careful planning.

- Providing benefits to employees should be instituted after careful review and planning involving qualified professionals.

- All roads to provide for healthcare needs of staff do not lead to tax-free benefits or penalty-free arrangements, and options should be carefully considered.

- Not all life insurance plans qualify as a "group" plan, so a church should take care to analyze any life insurance provided to a staff member to determine any taxable benefit.

- Disability insurance may be best provided as a taxable fringe benefit plan.

- Many options exist for assisting staff members with planning for retirement, and a church can select one that best fits their plans.

THE HOUSING ALLOWANCE

Understanding one of the most valuable benefits available to qualifying ministers

History

A parsonage (manse) is one of the oldest benefits provided to ministers by their churches. It dates back to 1921 when Congress decided it did not want to become entangled in church matters by examining any church's need for employer-provided housing to ministers. The exclusion from income tax for cash housing allowance was added with the 1954 revisions to the federal tax code. The additional exclusion equalized the treatment between ministers provided a home by the church and those who desired to own their own home.

Both methods of providing for a minister's housing are valuable. However, for many ministers the housing allowance is the most valuable benefit available to a minister—and it costs a church nothing to provide. Churches and ministers have increasingly opted for providing a housing allowance, rather than a parsonage due to the associated costs a parsonage presents to a church and the long-term benefits of home ownership by the minister. This shifting preference has been further encouraged by the increasingly mobile nature of American society, which has made it more common now for a minister to live outside the church's neighborhood.

Given its valuable nature, the housing allowance provision has faced repeated legal challenges in recent

ELAINE'S EXTRA

Despite recent legal challenges, ministers and churches may continue to utilize the housing allowance. However, it is wise to perform preliminary calculations to determine the financial effects of losing the housing allowance and be prepared for the additional costs, should an unfavorable outcome ultimately emerge at a national level.

years, with certain nonreligious groups contending it confers an unconstitutional preference for religion. During a 2002 case, the Ninth Circuit US Court of Appeals voiced its concern that the provision might violate the Establishment Clause of the First Amendment. But before the court could deliver a decision regarding the allowance, actions taken by Congress, the Internal Revenue Service, and the taxpayer involved with defending the allowance successfully shut down the Ninth Circuit's avenue of inquiry.[1]

Nevertheless, subsequent challenges still emerged, placing the question before other courts to debate and consider. The most recent legal challenge, brought before a federal district court in Wisconsin, resulted in a decision finding the housing allowance to be unconstitutional (the provision of a home by a church or the parsonage was not included in the case). The judge who handed down the decision, which would affect ministers and churches in Wisconsin, also entered an injunction ordering the IRS to disallow any minister from claiming benefits from the cash housing allowance provided by IRC Section 107(2). The injunction has been suspended while the case goes before the Seventh Circuit US Court of Appeals.[2] If upheld by the Seventh Circuit US Court of Appeals, the ruling would apply to ministers in Illinois, Indiana, and Wisconsin.

At the time of this book's publication, the appeal remained active. Churches in the affected states should still provide the benefit to their ministers, although they must watch for the appellate court's decision and respond accordingly, if necessary, when it comes.

Likewise, churches and ministers across the rest of the country also should continue to provide the benefit. However, all should note that the eventual appellate court decision could still go before the United States Supreme Court for review and a decision settling the matter once and for all (favorable or unfavorable, and establishing a national precedent binding on all states). Separately, were the Seventh Circuit to affirm the federal district judge's decision, and the Supreme Court opt not to review the case, the IRS could decide to apply the holding on a nationwide basis in order to maintain consistency with tax-related administration. The long-range outlook for the housing allowance remains unclear. Church leaders should stay up-to-date on this matter by regularly checking for developments on ChurchLawAndTax.com.

Benefits of the Parsonage/Housing Allowance

Internal Revenue Code Section 107 addresses providing parsonages and paying housing allowances. Under IRC Section 107(1), a minister may be provided a parsonage for his or her

---

[1] Warren v. Comm., 91 AFTR 2d 2003-2736 (282 F.3d 1119)
[2] Gaylor v. Mnuchin, 120 AFTR 2d 2017-6841 (DC WI)

use. Under IRC Section 107(2), the minister may request a portion of his or her compensation package to be designated as a housing allowance.

Either the parsonage or the housing allowance is desirable because of the beneficial tax provisions.

> *Federal Income Tax.* The housing allowance, subject to certain limitations, is excluded from federal income tax. Additionally, even though mortgage interest and taxes may be paid with the housing allowance, a minister may still claim these items as itemized deductions on Schedule A of his Form 1040. The ability to pay these items with tax-free dollars and still claim them as a deduction is commonly referred to as the "double deduction."

> The annual fair rental value of a church-provided parsonage is excluded from federal income tax.

> *Self-Employment Tax.* The housing allowance is subject to self-employment tax. The value of a provided parsonage is also subject to self-employment tax.

Taking full advantage of the federal tax benefits afforded to the parsonage and/or the housing allowance requires certain actions by both the church and the minister. Churches need to be fully aware of the role they play in providing this benefit to avoid undesirable consequences for a minister.

Actions Required by the Church

The church providing the benefit must take specific action. The following tax rules apply to the employing church:

- The recipient minister must possess a qualifying ministerial credential from a church and the minister must be performing ministerial duties. What constitutes ministerial duties is discussed in Chapter 6;

- Churches providing parsonages should designate the recipient minister through a formal designation process committed in writing;

- Before making a payment, churches providing

ELAINE'S EXTRA

Housing allowances should be documented each December for the upcoming calendar year. However, the amount of a housing allowance designation may be changed during a tax year for compensation amounts that have not been paid. Once compensation dollars have been paid, they may not be recharacterized from taxable salary to housing allowance.

housing allowances should determine and designate the amount of the housing allowance by an "official action" of the church. While verbal approvals have been allowed by the courts,[3] the proper "official action" of the church should be documented in writing. This may be accomplished through:

> › Written minutes of the appropriate governing body approving the decision;

> › In an employment contract detailing the amount provided;

> › In an approved budget detailing the amounts allocated to each minister; or

> › Through an internal written approval process of the church by the appropriate church representative.

To properly secure the benefits, the housing allowance should be formally designated in writing prior to the payment of the housing allowance.[4] The written documentation is not required to be a detail of the expected expenses, although this is common. (See page 171 for a sample housing allowance request form.) A documentation failure is an operational failure and may cost the minister the housing allowance;

• For churches providing a parsonage, a cash housing allowance may also be provided to cover any of a minister's out-of-pocket housing expenses. (It is required to be documented in the same manner as any other housing allowance);

• The housing allowance should <u>not</u> be reported as part of a minister's gross wages, either on Form 941 or Form W-2; and

• At the end of the tax year, the church should provide the amount of housing allowance paid to a minister, either through a letter or by listing it in Box 14 of Form W-2.

For ministers in a parsonage, the church should provide the minister with the fair rental value of the parsonage. This information normally is provided to the minister in a letter detailing the amount.

Example 11-1

Each year, in December, First Church reviews all of its employees to confirm which ones qualify as ministers for federal tax purposes. Qualifying ministers are requested to submit a form listing an estimate of their housing expenses and provide a formal request for a housing allowance. The personnel committee meets prior to the first payroll of the new year and approves the housing allowance requests. The approval of the housing allowance is noted in the minutes of the personnel committee meeting and the requests are

---

[3] Kizer v. Commissioner, T.C. Memo 1992-584
[4] IRC Section 107 & Logie v. Commissioner, T.C. Memo 1998-387

included as an attachment to the minutes. The requests are then provided to the payroll department and are filed in the ministers' personnel files. First Church has properly designated the housing allowances and documented these designations.

Example 11-2

Each year, in December, Second Church reviews all of its employees to confirm which ones qualify as ministers for federal tax purposes. Qualifying ministers are asked to submit a request for a housing allowance by any viable written method, such as e-mail. After reviewing the requests, the finance committee completes the annual budget, which includes the housing allowance for each minister separately stated as a line item in the budget. The budget is then approved at the annual church business meeting. Minutes of the church business meeting are recorded, and the budget with the detail of the housing allowance amounts is attached to the minutes. Second Church has properly designated and documented the housing allowance for its ministers.

Safety Net Allowances

Nothing is more distressful to a minister then finding out the church failed to designate a housing allowance for a given year. The consequences of failing to properly designate a housing allowance are costly, since no amount can be excluded from a minister's taxable income for a housing allowance without the designation. While designating the housing allowance annually is a best practice, a church may desire to include a safety net through the wording in the designation. This safety net would allow for the designation to remain in place for the upcoming year—and all future years—until changed. For example, the wording *"the housing allowance for 2019 and all future years, unless otherwise provided, is..."* would be included in the annual written designation of the housing allowance.

> **ELAINE'S EXTRA**
> Safety net designations provide a protection against accidental failures in properly designating a housing allowance. However, the best practice is to make an annual designation and not to depend upon a designation that is several years old.

Example 11-3

In March, at the quarterly personnel committee meeting, it is discovered that Pastor Joe's housing allowance designation for the current year was not submitted and approved prior to the start of the year. The payroll department did not make any changes to Pastor Joe's housing allowance and continued to pay the same amount in the current year as in the previous year. A review of the designation of the last housing allowance reveals the designation included both an amount and the provision for the amount to stay the same in all future years unless otherwise changed. Since a prior year's housing allowance designation included the safety net wording, Pastor Joe's housing allowance for the current year is still properly designated.

Guest or Interim Ministers

Churches may also designate a portion of an honorarium paid to a guest minister or an interim minister who provides services to the church. The church must determine the amount of the payment to be a housing allowance prior to providing the payment to the guest/interim minister. The church also should provide the designation in writing along with the payment to the guest/interim minister. Any amount of the honorarium designated as a housing allowance should not be included on the Form 1099-MISC issued to the guest/interim minister.

Actions Required by the Minister

Maximizing—and maintaining—the benefits of a housing allowance requires ministers to take certain steps in preparing their tax returns. Too many times the evaluation of the housing allowance stops with the designation and payment by the church. Ministers may mistakenly believe that the amount of the housing allowance paid is automatically tax-free. Ministers have the ultimate responsibility to properly report the housing allowance on their Form 1040, including determining if any housing allowance represents taxable income for federal income tax purposes.

Understanding the Limitations

Both ministers and tax preparers have to understand the limitations applied to the housing allowance. The amount of the housing allowance excluded from federal taxable income is the lesser of three limitations:

Limitation #1: The amount designated as housing allowance by the church.[5]

As previously discussed, it is the church's responsibility to properly designate a housing allowance for a minister. The amount of the properly designated housing allowance should be conveyed to the minister each year, either in a letter or in Box 14 of Form W-2.

Limitation #2: The amount spent on housing expenses during the calendar year.[6]

This is defined to be any amount spent to provide for a home [a dwelling place (including

---

[5] Treas. Reg. Sec. 1.107-1(b)
[6] IRC Sec. 107(2)

furnishings) and the appurtenances thereto.][7] This can include the following:

- Mortgage payment, including interest (the interest is still deductible on Schedule A with Form 1040);

- Mortgage payments on a home-equity mortgage or loan when the proceeds of the loan have been used on housing expenses;[8]

- Rent;

- Insurance;

- Taxes (the taxes are still deductible on Schedule A with Form 1040);

- Utilities;

- Landline phone—but not a cell phone;

- Lawn care and landscaping;

- Repairs and maintenance;

- Cleaning, but not including any services provided for the personal care of the family;

- Furnishings;

- Down payments; and

- Homeowner's association dues

> **ELAINE'S EXTRA**
> While housing expenses may include a down payment on a new home, a significant down payment will often cause the housing expenses to exceed the fair rental value of the home and will not provide any additional tax benefit. The same dollars may be able to be utilized in future years if included in the financing amount and paid through mortgage payments. Therefore, increasing the amount of the down payment may be detrimental to maximizing the use of the housing allowance.

As noted above, the housing allowance is intended to cover the expenses of the primary residence. Expenses **not** associated with providing a primary residence include:

- Expenses related to the property associated with the home that are additional to the "dwelling" purposes, such as a farm or other business property (such as a rental property);

- Expenses related to a home still owned by the minister when a job change requires the family to move to another area and occupy a new primary residence;

---

[7] Treas. Reg. Sec. 1.107-1(b)
[8] Rasmussen v. Commissioner, T.C. Memo 1994-311

- Expenses associated with a home under construction and not yet utilized for the primary residence; or

- Expenses used to calculate a home office deduction.

ELAINE'S EXTRA

The source for the fair rental value should be independent to the minister (i.e., it should not be provided by a relative, friend, or church member).

Limitation #3: The fair rental value of the home, as furnished, plus utilities.[9]

No guidance is provided by the IRS on the acceptable methodology for determining the fair rental value of a furnished home. The fair rental value may be determined using a real estate professional or by locating comparable published rental rates in the local area. The rental value should be reevaluated every three to five years, and the minister should obtain proof of the rental value, in writing, as part of his tax records.

Warning: *If a minister skips this step and is audited by the IRS, the IRS will go with any rental value they determine. Since IRS exams occur two to three years after a tax year, any value determined by the IRS may not reflect the true value existing in the tax year. If the real estate market has declined, this can be detrimental to the minister's tax calculation.*

Applying the Limitations

After determining the amounts described in the three limitations above, the amount of housing allowance excluded from federal income tax is the lowest of the three limitations. The amount of housing allowance received in excess of the lowest of the three limitations is taxable and is included on Line 7 of the minister's Form 1040. Documentation of each of the above limitations and the analysis to determine the taxable amount should be kept for three to six years after a minister's tax return is filed.

Example 11-4

First Church designates a housing allowance of $25,000 each year for Pastor Smith (limitation #1). In 2018, Pastor Smith spends $30,000 for housing expenses (limitation #2). Consulting with a local realtor, Pastor Smith determines the fair rental value of his home as furnished is $1,500 per month or $18,000 each year, and in 2018, Pastor Smith spent $3,000 on utilities (limitation #3). Even though Pastor Smith spent $30,000 for housing expenses and received a $25,000 housing allowance, the fair rental value of his house plus utilities is $21,000 (limitation #3). The fair rental value plus utilities is the

---

[9] IRC Sec. 107(2)

lowest amount, so Pastor Smith must include $4,000 (designated housing of $25,000 less fair rental value of $21,000) on his Form 1040, Line 7, as taxable income.

See page 164 for a sample form to use with evaluating the limitations and calculating the taxable amount. It is not necessary to attach a detailed calculation of the taxable portion of the housing allowance to Form 1040. However, many tax preparation software packages include a shortened calculation as a part of the Form 1040 schedules.

Warning: *If a housing allowance represents a substantial portion of a minister's income, then the income on the Form 1040 may be low, but the itemized deductions on Schedule A may be high. This results from the ability to deduct mortgage interest and taxes paid with the housing allowance. This imbalance may create additional scrutiny by the IRS. If the tax software utilized to prepare the tax return does not include information regarding the housing allowance as a part of its return statements, the following statement may be included as an attachment to the Form 1040.*

> *Taxpayer is a minister of the Gospel and a portion of his compensation has been designated as housing allowance under IRC Section 107. To the extent the housing allowance has been utilized to provide his residence and does not exceed the fair rental value, as defined in IRC Section 107(2), it has been excluded from income. Excess housing allowance, if any, has been reported on Line 7 of Form 1040. The total amount of the housing allowance has been included in income for purposes of calculating self-employment tax on Schedule SE. (For ministers exempt from self-employment tax, the last sentence of the above paragraph may be omitted from the statement.)*

Housing Allowance Myths

There are a number of myths about the housing allowance available to ministers.

Myth #1: The church should determine if the minister has any taxable income from the housing allowance by asking for an accounting of his expenses before his Form W-2 is prepared.

> **Reality:** While this method is available, it is not in the best interest of the church to create an actual exclusion method of reporting the housing allowance. Following this method requires the church to determine too many variables affecting taxable income. The church must determine the legitimate housing expenses as well as the fair rental value of a home as furnished. Few churches are qualified to provide the analysis sufficiently to attest to the taxable portion of the housing allowance for reporting on Form W-2. It is not the

obligation of the church to make sure a minister excludes the correct amount from his or her taxable income. If a church follows this method and assists a minister in claiming too much housing allowance, effectively understating the minister's taxable income, then it could find itself open to a charge of assisting a minister in evading income taxes, at the worst, or reimbursing for penalties and interest charged to a minister for underreporting income. Therefore, it is not recommended the church ask for documentation of a minister's housing expenses at the end of the year to determine if there is a taxable amount to be reported on the Form W-2.

Myth #2: Housing allowances can be used for more than one house.

Reality: Housing is allowed for the principal residence and only one residence at a time.[10] Additionally, it may only be used for a reasonable portion of land or other property associated with the residence and not for an extended piece of land and/or buildings utilized for other purposes.

Myth #3: The housing allowance can only be a set percentage of a minister's total cash compensation package.

Reality: There is no set percentage of how much of the compensation package can be allocated to the housing allowance. It is possible for 100 percent of the cash compensation to be allocated to housing allowance. This is a common practice with bi-vocational ministers. However, designating 100 percent of cash compensation as housing allowance may affect participation in other fringe benefit plans, including retirement plan, or restrict provisions for voluntary withholding of taxes by the minister.

Myth #4: A minister can select his own housing allowance on his tax return.

Reality: Without a designation from a qualifying employer (i.e., the church), a minister does not have a housing allowance. He or she may not choose an amount as a housing allowance when filing his or her Form 1040.

---

[10] Driscoll v. Commissioner, 2012 U.S. App. LEXIS 2403 (11th Cir. 2012).

CHAPTER 11 KEY POINTS:

- The housing allowance is still a valuable benefit available for ministers.

- The church must designate the housing allowance in writing and in advance of payment.

- The minister must determine if any portion of the housing allowance is taxable when he or she prepares an individual income tax return.

APPENDIX

Summary of Taxation of Common Forms of Compensation

Type of Compensation	IRC Section	FIT	SE Tax Ministers	FICA	Medi-care	Formal Written Plan Required	$ Limitations	Comments
Basic Forms of Cash Pay								
Base Salary/Wages Paid	61(a)(1)	x	x	x	x			
Bonuses Paid	61(a)(1)	x	x	x	x			
Special Occassion Gifts	61(a)(1)/102	x	x	x	x			
Money Tree Funds	61(a)(1)	x	x	x	x			
Incentive Compensation	61(a)(1)	x	x	x	x			
Tax Gross Ups Paid	61(a)(1)	x	x	x	x			
Gift Cards	61(a)(1)	x	x	x	x			
Intern Support	61(a)(1)	x	x	x	x			
SE Tax Reimbusements or Supplements	61(a)(1)	x	x	N/A	N/A			
Any Cash or Noncash Gifts	61(a)(1)/102	x	x	x	x			Only small inexpensive noncash items would be tax-free.

Type of Compensation	IRC Section	FIT	SE Tax Ministers	FICA	Medi-care	Formal Written Plan Required	$ Limitations	Comments
Fringe Benefits - Health Plans								
Vacation/Sick Leave Paid Out	105(a)/409A	x	x	x	x	x		
Health Insurance Premiums	106							While they may still be tax-free, the ACA only allows paying for group insurance plan premiums without a penalty to the church.
Participation in medical sharing arrangements	106	x	x	x	x			These payments are not for insurance and are taxable unless used as a component of an employer's self-insured plan.

Summary of Taxation of Common Forms of Compensation *(continued)*

Type of Compensation	IRC Section	FIT	SE Tax Ministers	FICA	Medi-care	Formal Written Plan Required	$ Limitations	Comments
Health Reimbursement Account for out-of-pocket medical expenses	106					x	x	ACA rules limit the use of these plans. Small employer plans have dollar limitations in addition to other limitations.
Disability insurance	106	?	?	?	?			Taxation of the premium may be optional.
Health Savings Accounts	106					x	x	

Fringe Benefits - Transportation								
Flat auto allowances	61(a)(1)	x	x	x	x			
Payment of auto expenses	61(a)(1)	x	x	x	x			
Employer provided auto - personal portion	Treas. Reg. 1.61-21	x	x	x	x			Failure to document the business use results in 100% of the use being personal use.
Qualified transportation benefits such as employer provided parking	132(f)					x	x	Limits are established each year.
Flights on employer aircraft - personal flights	Treas. Reg. 1.61-21	x	x	x	x			

Fringe Benefits - Education								
Scholarships	117(a)	?	?	?	?	x		Plans benefiting only employees may not represent a qualified scholarship program and may be taxable to the recipient.
Fellowship Work Grants	117(c)	x	x	x	x			
Educational assistance for higher education of employees	127					x	x	Plans limited to $5,250 per year.

Summary of Taxation of Common Forms of Compensation *(continued)*

Type of Compensation	IRC Section	FIT	SE Tax Ministers	FICA	Medi-care	Formal Written Plan Required	$ Limitations	Comments
Tuition reduction for school employees and their dependents	117(d)					x		
Tuition payments for employees' dependents outside of a tuition reduction plan	61(a)(1)	x	x	x	x			
Continuing education to meet work requirements	132							

Fringe Benefits - Personal Life Benefits								
Life Insurance outside of group plan	79	x	x	x	x			
Life insurance with a group plan	79					x	x	Tax-free portion is limited to $50,000 of coverage.
Key man life insurance								
Housing allowance	107(2)		x	N/A	N/A	x		Designate in writing and in advance.
Parsonage	107(1)		x	N/A	N/A			
Housing provided to lay employees	119	?	N/A	?	?			Housing provided as a requirement to perform job duties may be tax-free.
Personal legal services						x	x	
Dependent care assistance	129					x	x	Plans limited to $5,000 per year.
Adoption assistance	137		x	x	x	x	x	Plans limited to $13, 840 with phaseouts for persons in higher income brackets.
Moving expenses	217/132(g)	x	x	x	x			Effective 1/1/2018.
Social club dues	274	?	?	?	?			Requires an allocation based on use of the club for church purposes.
Health club dues	274	x	x	x	x			

Summary of Taxation of Common Forms of Compensation (continued)

Type of Compensation	IRC Section	FIT	SE Tax Ministers	FICA	Medi-care	Formal Written Plan Required	$ Limitations	Comments
Payment of personal expenses such as weddings	61(a)(1)	X	X	X	X			
Clothing suitable for street wear	262(a)	X	X	X	X			
Fees for family members to attend camps or conferences	61(a)(1)	X	X	X	X			
Loans		?	?	?	?			Most states forbid the making of a loan to a director of a nonprofit organization.
Loans - forgone interest/ debt forgiveness	61(a)(1)	X	X	X	X			Only in limited instances is this an acceptable practice.
Fringe Benefits - Work Related								
Travel for spouses and family members without business purpose	61(a)(1)/274/132	X	X	X	X			
Travel advances without subsequent documentation	274	X	X	X	X			
Reimbursements through an accountable plan	62(a)					X		
Reimbursements through a nonaccountable plan	62(c)	X	X	X	X			
Discretionary accounts with no accountability	62 & 274	X	X	X	X			
Employee Discounts	132						X	Limitations apply based on the discount being offered.
Qualified transportation costs	132					X	X	Limitations apply based on the benefit offered to the employee.
Forms of Termination and/or Retirement Plans								
Severance Pay	61(a)(1) & 409A	X	X	X	X			

Summary of Taxation of Common Forms of Compensation *(continued)*

Type of Compensation	IRC Section	FIT	SE Tax Ministers	FICA	Medi-care	Formal Written Plan Required	$ Limitations	Comments
Contributions (employer) to qualified retirement plan	401/403					x	x	Generally limited to $55,000 in 2018 with limitations based on taxable income and various catch up additions available. Limits are indexed each year.
Contributions (employee elective deferral) to qualified retirement plan	401/403			x	x	x	x	Generally limited to $18,500 in 2018 with limitations based on taxable income and various catch-up additions available. Limits are indexed each year.
Contributions to a SEP-IRA				x	x	x	x	Limited to 25% of income or $55,000.
Elective deferrals of contributions to a Simple IRA				x	x	x	x	Limited to $12,500 with a catch-up for over age 50 of $3,000.
Contributions to IRAs outside of a SEP-IRA or a Simple IRA	401	x	x	x	x			
Contributions to nonqualified deferred compensation plans	409A	?	?	?	?	x		Seek professional assistance in developing these plans.
Qualified Retirement Planning Services	132(a)(7)							
Payments from nonqualified deferred compensation plans	409A	x	Not if a retirement plan payment	x	x	x		

Comparison of Educational Assistance Plans & Continuing Education Plans

Providing for employees' education expenses is gaining popularity among employers. These benefits provide employers with a way to retain valuable staff members as well as invest in their skills. There are two methods for employers to provide educational expenses for employees.

- IRC Section 127 allows an employer to create and maintain an educational assistance plan. These plans may cover expenses for virtually any field of study other than athletics.
- IRC Section 132 allows an employer to pay for expenses that are incurred to keep its employees educated in areas that benefit their jobs and/or are required to maintain their jobs.

The two plans have different requirements and serve two different purposes. The plans are not interchangeable, and an employer may have one of the plans or could maintain both plans. The following table summarizes the two plans as to their benefits and their requirements.

Factor/Benefit	Sec. 127 Educational Assistance Plan	Sec. 132 Continuing Educational Plan
Written plan document required	Yes	No[i]
Required to provide notice of plan availability to all eligible employees	Yes	No
Required to be a nondiscriminatory plan	Yes[ii]	No
May have provision requiring continued employment	Yes	Yes
May require proof of successful completion of courses to obtain benefits	Yes	Yes
Plan can offer either an education benefit or cash in lieu of the benefit	No	No
Expenses required to be considered as deductible by the employee under Sec. 162 as a business expense to be considered for the plan	No	Yes
Expenses required to be related to maintaining or improving skills required for current job or employment	No	Yes
Benefits paid through the plan are generally tax-free to the employee	Yes	Yes
Taxable benefit if required to meet the minimum educational requirements for qualification in the employee's employment or business	No	Yes[iii]
Taxable if part of a program of study will qualify the employee to engage in a new trade or business or receive a different position with the current employer	No	Yes[iv]
Expenses allowed for tuition, fees, books, supplies, and equipment	Yes	Yes
Expenses allowed for meals, lodging, and transportation	No	Yes
Expenses allowed for a bachelor's or a master's degree	Yes	Yes[v]
Expenses allowed for doctoral degree	Yes	No[vi]
Limited in amount of benefit	Yes - $5,250	No
Expenses allowed for tools and supplies that may be retained by the employee after the completion of a course	No	No
Substantiation required for reimbursement of allowed expenses	Yes	Yes[vii]

i   Most commonly a part of the employer's business expense documentation and reimbursement policy.

ii   Cannot discriminate in favor of highly compensated as defined in 414(q), and current definition for 2018 is $120,000. If there are persons meeting this definition, then a classification has to be tested to determine if it is reasonable and whether it creates a discriminatory plan. (Effective with the 1986 Tax Reform Act, officers are no longer an automatic part of the discrimination testing. Reg. Sec. 1.127-2(e)(1) is out of date.)

iii   Generally, a bachelor's degree of any kind may be considered a minimum requirement of the employer or qualifying a person for a new job.

iv   A change in duties in the employment arrangement is not a new trade or business, if the new duties involve substantially the same type of work as the employee has been involved in for the employer. The courts emphasize the duties or jobs that the employee obtains after the education is completed leading to a 20/20 hindsight test that might not be clear at the time the education is obtained.

v   Great weight is given as to whether the student is still gainfully employed in his/her profession at the time of the education and if the education is simply enhancing those employment skills. The courts emphasize the duties or jobs that the employee obtains after the education is completed leading to a 20/20 hindsight test that might not be clear at the time the education is obtained. Because any education leading to a degree may be considered as qualifying an employee for a new job, many continuing education plans exclude these courses to avoid potential complications in administering the plan.

vi   In general, obtaining a doctoral degree will qualify an employee for a new trade or business, even if the employee does not pursue that trade or business.

vii   Substantiation for travel expenses includes all lodging receipts and receipts for meals expenses of $75 or more.

Minister's Housing Allowance: Calculating the Taxable Portion

This form may be used by ministers in calculating the taxable portion of their housing allowance, if any, received during the year. The form may also be modified to be used by churches to have ministers estimate housing expenses to request housing allowance designations by the church.

Calculation of Taxable Housing Allowance Included in Line 7 of Form 1040	
Line 1: Housing Allowance Designated and Paid to Minister	$
Line 2: Housing Allowance Paid During Tax Year	
Line 2a - Primary Housing Expenses	
Mortgage - Principal & Interest	$
Real Estate Taxes	$
Insurance	$
Repairs	$
Security Systems	$
Furnishings	$
Home equity loan payments *	$
Household, i.e., cleaning supplies, services, and décor items	$
Pool costs	$
Landscape and other yard expenses	$
Down payment or other home purchase costs	$
Total Line 2a	$
Line 2b - Utilities	
Electric	$
Water/Sewer	$
Gas	$
Home Land Line Telephone**	$
Total Line 2b	$
Total Line 2 (Lines 2a and 2b)	$
Line 3: Fair Rental Value Limitation	
Rental value of residence***	$
Rental value of furnishings (if not included in residence's rental value) ***	$
Utilities from Line 2b	$
Total Line 3	$
Line 4: List the lowest value of Line 1; Line 2; or Line 3	$
Line 5: Taxable Portion of Housing Allowance - Line 1 minus Line 4 (If less than -0- enter -0-)	$

* Home equity loan payments may be used as housing expenses if the loan proceeds were used to pay for housing expenses not claimed in the year of purchase.

** Cell phones expenses may not be used as housing expenses.

*** There is no guidance on how to determine the rental value of a furnished home. Documentation from a third party to support these calculations should be kept. Reaffirm rental values every three to four years.

[Name of Church]
Employer Provided Cell Phone Policy

[Name of church] has agreed to provide *[name of employee]* with a cell phone (or a cash reimbursement when phones are personally owned by the employee) as a working condition fringe benefit as allowed under IRC Section 132. The cell phone, including any related data plans, is a tool that will enable *[name of employee]* to fully perform and fulfill his/her employment duties to *[name of church]* and is not being provided as additional compensation for the performance of his/her duties. Therefore, any personal use will be considered as a de minimis fringe benefit and not included in *[name of employee]'s* taxable income.

[Name of church] believes that a cell phone (or cash reimbursement), that includes data plans, may be provided for non-compensatory reasons to the above-mentioned employee based on one or more of the following business reasons:

___ The employee's duties require him/her to be available at all times to the management and members of *[name of church]*.[1]

___ The employee's duties require communication, on a regular basis, with persons in other parts of the world that may not be on the same timetable as [name of locale].

___ The employee's duties consistently require travel on behalf of *[name of church]* away from the church's offices on a regular basis.

___ The employee's duties are involved in the conduct of meetings, conferences, and conventions that will require the employee to communicate with either the church's office or with others onsite at the meeting venue in order to effectively accomplish a successful ministry program.

___ The employee's duties require him/her to work at various locations at the church's campuses that do not have ready phone access.

Considering the above noted business reasons for the need for mobile communication abilities, the employee is being provided:

___ A cell phone that is purchased by *[name of church]* and is a part of *[name of church]'s* telephone plan; or

___ A cash allowance of $ _____ will be paid with proof that *[name of employee]* is incurring an actual expense equal to or greater than the cash allowance.

_____

[Name of church] representative

_____

Date

---

[1] Care should be taken with this option. It should only be checked for employees that meet the ministerial exception or are classified as an exempt employee for wage and hour rules. Checking this option for a nonexempt employee may create an on-call employee and require wage compensation for 24 hours a day. See Chapter 5 for a further discussion of this topic.

25659389R00096

Made in the USA
Columbia, SC
02 September 2018